FORDS OF THE FIFTIES

Michael Parris

California Bill's
Automotive Handbooks

Publishers
Bill Fisher
Helen V. Fisher
Howard W. Fisher

Editor
Ron Sessions

Cover and Interior Design
Gary D. Smith, Performance Design

Cover Photography
Michael Parris

Interior Photography
Michael Parris unless otherwise noted

Published by
California Bill's Automotive Handbooks
P.O. Box 91858
Tucson, AZ 85752
520-744-6110

Distributed by
Motorbooks International
729 Prospect Avenue
PO Box 1
Osceola, WI 54020-0001
800-826-6600

ISBN
1-931128-14-6

Printed in the United States of America

1 2 3 4 5 6 7 8 9 10 - 03 02 01 00

We would like to thank Henry Ford Museum and Greenfield Village and Ford Motor Company for the use of photos from their collections, appearing under the captions of "Henry Ford Museum and Ford Motor Company" through chapter eight, and under the captions of "Ford Motor Company" in chapters nine through 15.

**Library of Congress
Cataloging-in-Publication Data**

Parris, Michael.
    Fords of the Fifties / Michael Parris.
    p. cm.
    Includes index.
    ISBN 1-931128-14-6
    1. Ford automobile-History. I. Title.

    TL215.F7 P36 2000
    629.222'2-dc21   00-034818
                        CIP

Contents

Car Owner Acknowledgments

Classic car owners spend endless hours restoring their vehicles just to enjoy driving them, showing them at car shows and sharing a bit of nostalgia with people everywhere. The owners listed here have gone beyond the call of duty and driven many miles to have their vehicles photographed for this book and I would like to offer thanks to each one of them for their efforts. I have made many good friends during the process of writing about these historic Fords and this book could not have been published without their support and cooperation.

California
Jim Cain	'57 Custom 300
Don Driver	'56 Fordor
Jerry Johnson	'50 Tudor
Dan Kaiser	'54 Sunliner
Richard Kemph	'50 Fordor
Wayne MacCartney	'59 Retractable
John Murray	'57 Retractable, '52 Convertible
Mitch Reed	'56 Meteor Victoria
Gary & Linda Richards	'55 Tudor
Wayne Simpkin	'50 Convertible

Michigan
Bob Bell	'52 Victoria
Tom Brownlee	'55 T-Bird
Maurice Cash	'51 Convertible
Jim Chapp	'55 Crown Victoria
Steve Farley	'56 Crown Victoria, '56 Victoria
Frank Fitzgerald	'51 Country Squire wagon
Bob Haas	'54 Sunliner, '56 Crown Victoria
Larry Haase	'58 Retractable, '50 Club Coupe, '55 T-Bird
Vic Hollingshead	'49 Club Coupe
Mel Kaftan	'56 Sunliner
Mark Kirby	'53 Fordor
Jim Kunath	'58 Thunderbird
Gene Machinski	'55 Skyliner
Jerry Mills	'49 Convertible
Joe Mooradian	'53 Sunliner Pace Car
Don & Sandy Olson	'51 Tudor
Mark Schwartz	'57 Sunliner
Todd Skolnicki	'54 Victoria
Doug Shull	'50 F-1 pickup
Ken Vanniman	'56 Victoria, '56 Crown Victoria
Howard Voigt	'58 & '59 Retractable Fords
Dan Waller	'53 Sunliner

New Zealand
Martin Barratt	'57 RHD Country Wagon & '58 Fairlane
Chris Leigh	New Zealand auto collection
Tony & Kelly Meester	'56 Crown Victoria & '56 RHD Fordor
David & Karen Warman	'58 RHD Custom 300

Acknowledgments

Writing a book takes an abundance of time—time away from your hobbies, leisure and especially away from your family. While this may not top *The York New Times* bestseller list, it is a labor of love that will hopefully find its way into the hands of those who understand and love automobiles. Working many late hours writing text and capturing classic cars on film takes the understanding of those closest to you and my family has always given their support and understanding. This book is dedicated to the girls in my life: my wife Heidi, daughters Erin and Allison and our trusty 12-pound guard dog, Abby. They're the best.

Research also absorbs much of a writer's time and the cooperation of information sources is invaluable. Working with Elizabeth Adkins at the Ford Motor Company Archives, the Henry Ford and Greenfield Village Museum archives, The Detroit Library's *National Automotive Collection* and the American Automobile Manufacturers' Association archives was an experience in developing not only professional business relationships but many friendships as well.

And the workhorse team that really makes the book come together would have to include Howard Fisher for his publishing leadership, Gary Smith for his untiring creative design work and my friend Ron Sessions for hours of editing all the details.

Introduction

 The decade was the '50s, one of the most nostalgic periods in the 20th century. Eisenhower was president, Marilyn Monroe married former baseball star Joe DiMaggio and Elvis was taking the youth of the country by storm. Cars and trucks were enjoying huge sales and offered great styling compared to pre-war models. America was back on the road in a big way and was enjoying spending money in a robust economy. This included everything from kitchen appliances and televisions to shag carpeting and cars with fins.

The Ford Motor Company found itself at a pivotal point at the close of World War II. It was coming out from under the rule of Henry Ford and henchman Harry Bennett on the brink of disaster as it transferred power into the hands of young Henry Ford II, grandson of the founder.

The company's debts were so out of control that the accounting department was guessing at how much they owed creditors by measuring the height of a stack of invoices.

Any story about Ford during the 1950s would have to include the development of not only the all-important 1949 Ford but also the company's restructuring as it dealt with huge financial losses, low sales performance, labor problems and the lingering effects of World War II.

Building new automobiles would not be possible without first changing the way Ford ran its business—and that would mean a total reorganization. During the mid-1940s, Ford was in third place behind General Motors and Chrysler and it lacked any exciting new products or the leadership to develop a sound plan for its future. Things weren't looking good.

This story began in 1945 with Henry Ford II and Ernie Breech, the key men who would develop Henry Ford's company into a new success story during the coming decade. They had no choice but to participate in risk-taking of gigantic proportions while creating a vision, a well-oiled organization and a new product line to capture the imagination of the nation. It would be a challenge.

▶

Henry Ford II, at the time executive vice president of Ford Motor Company, autographs the last of 8,685 B-24 "Liberator" bombers produced by the company on June 28, 1945, at the Willow Run (Michigan) plant. In the U.S. war effort, Ford Motor Company produced, in addition to the B-24s, 57,000 aircraft engines and over 250,000 jeeps, tanks, tank destroyers and other pieces of war machinery—all in less than three years. (Photo: Henry Ford Museum and Ford Motor Company)

FIRE EXTINGUISHER

1 • *Laying the Foundation*

FORD

Shortly before his death, Henry Ford threw in his support for his grandson, Henry II, to become president of Ford Motor Company. This was the last nod young Henry needed to take over the company and move Henry's henchman, Harry Bennett, out the door. (Photo: Henry Ford Museum and Ford Motor Company)

Laying the Foundation

It was April 2, 1948, and three men working on the assembly line at Ford Motor Company's famous Rouge Plant were posing for a photo for the Rouge News, the largest of the Ford employee newspapers. It showed them assembling one of the first 1949 pilot-model sedans, happy to be back at work after being laid off during "changeover" for the new models. Ford now had a well-received post-war design to bring the company back from the brink and, under the guidance of Henry Ford II and executive vice president Ernie Breech, had what appeared to be a bright future for the 1950s. But Ford's future hadn't always been that bright.

During the prior ten years, aging company founder Henry Ford had turned much control of the company over to his lieutenant, Harry Bennett, and Ford was losing as much as $10 million per month in the early 1940s. The car designs were falling further and further behind both General Motors and Chrysler. Ford was selling cars based on price, not customer enthusiasm. Henry's son, Edsel, was president of Ford Motor Company and had a deep love of cars, their design and the business of making and selling them, but wanted nothing to do with the rough and tumble

politics of the company. There were many who thought much of the turmoil and the overbearing attitude of old Henry contributed to Edsel's early death.

Henry Ford II, grandson of Henry Ford, returned from the Navy upon the death of his father, Edsel Ford, in 1943. The U.S. Government realized that young Henry's 81-year-old grandfather was in failing health and wanted to assure that a Ford was in the driver's seat. Ford production was essential to the war effort and they didn't feel comfortable that all would be well with the senior Ford back in the presidency. J.R. Davis, head of Ford Division, later commented that when young Henry Ford II came in, "the company was not only dying, it was already dead, and rigor mortis was setting in." Young Henry Ford recognized that cleaning house of Bennett and his men should be the first order of business.

He accomplished this within a week of taking over the presidency on September 21, 1945. It wasn't an easy task, one that had taken almost two years of planning since coming home from the Navy. Henry II worked quietly behind the scenes to build alliances within the company and gain the support of his mother and grandmother. Eventually his grandfather signed a letter of support, asking the board of directors to elect his grandson to the post of president, Ford Motor Company. He would need to start thinking about building a new team to lead the various operations within Ford. Henry II realized that he didn't have all the answers and started looking for strong leaders who did. A July 14, 1948, *Life* magazine article, "The New Ford," characterized young Henry as "going to work like a man on a ship leaking water in a dozen places. In less than a week he fired First Mate Bennett and began hiring new hands..."

Crossing the country, Henry II proceeded to fire somewhere between several hundred and a thousand workers with close ties to Bennett. At only 29 years old, many corporate leaders were wondering who his advisers were, but as one person close to the operation said, "I think Henry II's principal adviser is the memory of his father." He was young, sharp and tough when he needed to be.

New Leadership

The "Kids"

In late 1945, while building a new management team, Henry Ford II received a telegram from a group of ten Army Air Force officers fresh out of the service asking for an audience with him. The group, led by Charles "Tex" Thornton, was being offered to Ford as a package—all or none. Each had an area of expertise ranging from finance, business, law or teaching and came from all over the United States. The men, ranging in age from 26 to 34, offered diversity of experience, leadership, youthful enthusiasm and some of the best young minds around. This appealed to Henry II, who felt the need for some young faces to work with him in reforming Ford Motor Company. After an intense interviewing process, he hired them.

The new team became known as the "Quiz Kids" because their first four-month assignment was to visit virtually every area of the company and ask questions both to familiarize them with the automotive industry and to give them an idea of what kind of task lay ahead. Many employees were afraid the "kids" were hired as hatchet men to rid Ford of unwanted staff. What the young new team found was a financial disaster—records in total disarray,

with no prospect of getting better. They had a big job ahead.

After the new group had asked all their questions and began helping to reorganize the way the company did much of its business, they finally shed the "Quiz Kids" title, which most of them disliked, and became known as the Whiz Kids. Out of the original ten members, six went on to become vice presidents at Ford and two, Arjay Miller and Robert McNamara, served as presidents. McNamara later served as Secretary of Defense in the Kennedy administration.

By late 1945, Ford Motor Company was just coming out of the World War II government ban on domestic production and trying to develop better relations with the United Auto Workers (UAW) over workers' rights. Henry II made a speech to the Society of Automotive Engineers (SAE) in January, 1946, calling for unions and management to work together, coming to agreement in the same fashion as two

companies working out a contract. Although Ford's speech effectively legitimized the union, Ford also called for union heads to accept the social obligations that go with leadership. His speech was well accepted by the unions and management alike, and although there would be many strikes and labor hurdles in future years, it was the beginning of a better relationship between Ford and the unionized workforce.

Henry Ford also went a step further to mend the corporate relationship with workers in the plants. He had a survey sent to all plant employees asking questions such as, "Are you made to feel that you are a definite part of the company—a member of the Ford team? Do you believe that you are given a fair opportunity to make suggestions and criticisms about company practices and officials? How do you think the products of the Ford Motor Company compare with those of its principal competitors? Please be frank."

With Henry II in his late 20s, he hired Ernie Breech from GM's Bendix division to take over as executive vice president of Ford. Breech's organization and business skills, along with Henry's determination to bring change to the company, put Ford back on the right track. (Photo: Henry Ford Museum and Ford Motor Company)

Henry Ford II loved getting to know his employees. Visiting the Rouge complex fascinated him and he often made visits to get to know the people and the product. He took over the presidency of Ford Motor Company on September 21, 1945, at the age of 28. (Photo: Henry Ford Museum and Ford Motor Company)

Ford received an amazingly good 20 percent return to the survey that finally started a dialogue between management and workers after years of division. Henry II and his labor chief, John Bugas, were key in setting a tone of honesty when Ford went to the union bargaining table. Bugas, once head of the Detroit FBI office, was given full authority to make decisions when working with the UAW. This usually led to a fairly quick settlement, because the two sides could get right to business without the usual tactical dances. According to a 1947 *Fortune* magazine article, bargaining was hard and unsentimental, but was genuine, collective bargaining. Then-UAW Ford department head Dick Leonard said of Bugas, "They don't throw us any curves."

Henry's Partner

Ernie Breech, son of a Missouri blacksmith, began his career as comptroller of the Yellow Cab Manufacturing Company a year after getting his CPA. Later, when General Motors bought the car manufacturing company, Breech became a vice president of the household appliance divisions and later took over Bendix Aviation as president. He had approached Ford Motor Company about buying automotive parts from Bendix in the past, but with his GM association could never get his foot in the door. When he heard that the old guard was out and young Henry's team was in, he made another trip, hoping to start supplying Ford with parts. Henry II, on the other hand, was shopping for a mentor and a seasoned businessman to reorganize the way Ford Motor Company ran its total operations.

Soon after Breech walked in the door, Henry II had an idea that this could be the man he was looking for. He had heard about Breech's reputation as a troubleshooter, restructuring poorly running operations into profitable houses.

Young Henry desperately needed someone who could restructure the company and set processes in place to build better cars. Breech's financial background and comprehensive understanding of the automotive industry was what Ford was after.

Henry II decided he would offer Breech an executive vice president's title and the authority to completely rework how Ford operated. But Ernie Breech turned down the job flatly, being quite happy to run the Bendix operation, but said he would be glad to give the young Henry advice and help him as much as was possible. He didn't want to lose the Ford business for Bendix, but on the other hand, he really didn't want to take on Ford's mammoth problems either. In Breech's biography, *Ernie Breech*, he said, "While doing this I became more and more involved. One day, I asked to see the company's books, and well, that did it. The company was really in a mess. Not only did it need help, it had to have help or the Big Three would surely become the Surviving Two."

Considering that Breech was being groomed to head Chevrolet, it was quite a brave and risky move when he finally cut all ties with GM to accept the Ford offer. Henry had kept after him to take the position, offering him stock options, more salary than he made at Bendix and job security. Breech said that if he hadn't taken on this challenge to rebuild Ford Motor Company he would always have regretted it.

On July 1, 1946, Ernie Breech officially became a Ford employee and learned more of the problems facing him. Ford was losing $10 million per month and the company had no controls in place to show where and why it was losing the money. Old Henry had invested in nonautomotive-related businesses, such as Brazilian rubber plantations, soybean plants, timber acreage and other odds and ends that had been losing money for years. Breech shed the company of these negative cash-flow businesses and proceeded to put a decentralized form of management in place, similar to what Alfred P. Sloan had done with GM in the mid-1920s. This would show management exactly where the money was being spent and where the losses were occurring. Until this could be accomplished, the company would never be able to compete with the likes of General Motors.

While Ernie Breech was still at Bendix, his two sons had been awarded a new Chevrolet franchise in Birmingham, Michigan, and were about to send invitations for the grand opening when their father announced his departure to Ford. They both felt it would be an embarrassment to their father to run the Chevy store, and proceeded to liquidate and get cleanly out of the business before even opening the doors. Breech's close-knit family was obviously 100 percent behind his radical career change.

Under his agreement with Henry Ford, Breech (known as the "quarterback" inside Ford) brought four outside executives with him. They included L. D. Crusoe (planning and control), Harold Youngren (engineering), Del Harder (operations) and James Irwin (public relations).

L. D. Crusoe had retired from GM at age 50 to raise cattle in Michigan but came back into the business a year later to work as Breech's assistant at Bendix Aviation. Being an ex-GM Fisher Body Division executive, Crusoe thought that going to work at Ford was akin to going to work for the Red Army, but he agreed to try it with Breech and joined Ford in July of 1946. He had a thorough understanding of the automotive business and how to make a company run smoothly. He would become the ignition key to Ford's future.

Breech brought Harold Youngren over from the chief engineering position at Borg-Warner. Youngren too was an ex-GM man who had led the Oldsmobile Division's engineering team. He would prove instrumental in revitalizing Ford engineering during the 1950s.

Harder and Irwin were also key to the Ford rebuild, but not as vital initially as Crusoe and Youngren, who had to get costs under control and build a new car in record time.

It was Crusoe who finally got the first clue of what was wrong. Within the first two months on the job he found that Ford was losing $62 per car on manufacturing costs alone. Breech talked to Washington to get the price controls from the war lifted to cover these losses. He also set about cutting their money-losing businesses and trimming costs to bring the company back to a break-even situation. This allowed them to focus on the next task— quickly designing and building an all-new car to compete with Chevrolet's coming post-war model.

Ford's insider information said that Chevrolet would have their first post-war model out by 1947, so the company charged ahead on an 18-month crash program to design and produce a clean-sheet vehicle. As it turned out, Chevrolet was late getting out their model, and Ford's mid-1948 introduction was ahead of Chevy's by six months.

Another key player was purchasing head Albert Browning. Browning had been brigadier general in charge of all the Army's purchasing and contracts and was an ideal candidate to centralize Ford's purchasing operations. By working with the companies supplying parts for Ford's cars, Browning developed from their suggestions ways to save between $10 million and $20 million a year. His comment on the relationship was, "We're using our suppliers' products, why not use their brains?" On top of saving the company money, it also strengthened the bond with the suppliers.

Some of the money-saving ideas included making steering wheels in one color and without fancy trim; savings: $95,000 per year. Changing the type of bearing used in the clutch saved $310,000, a new type of door lock replacing a complicated one saved $569,000 and a special steel "speed nut" to speed up assembly on the line netted an astonishing $1 million or so in savings annually.

V-8? Not in the Plans

Early Product Planning

Before the late 1940s, Ford Motor Company had no product-planning department. Until 1947, engineering always told the company what would be built and the sales department didn't have much to say about it. Chase Morsey, a young employee with the company for only a few weeks, was given a book already approved by Youngren, Breech and Crusoe outlining details of the yet-to-be-introduced 1949 model. He was asked to review it as a part of his learning process at the company. Reviewing the book, Morsey soon realized that only a six-cylinder engine was slated for production—no V-8. Morsey said, "So I went back in to my boss Jack (Davis) and said, 'Jack, this will break the company. The V-8 is the Ford car. I'm a Ford guy and the V-8 is what makes people buy Fords.' So he said, 'OK, let's go in and see Mr. Crusoe.'"

L. D. Crusoe listened to Morsey's remarks on the V-8 deletion from the Forty-Niner and said, "Do you mean to tell me that after being in the business for six or eight weeks you think you know more about this than I do?" Staring him down, Crusoe said, "After my 30 years' experience, and all of Mr. Breech's experience and Mr. Youngren who was chief engineer at General Motors—you think you know more about this than we do?" A very nervous Morsey said, "Mr. Crusoe, I have one thing that all you guys don't have. I was a Ford owner, I love Ford cars and I know what makes a Ford go." Finally, Crusoe said, "OK, I'll go talk to Mr. Breech, but he'll be mad as hell." And according to Morsey, Breech was indeed "mad as hell" that a decision of this magnitude was being questioned at such a late date. He gave them 90 days to go

to the public and initiate Ford's first market research.

Ford didn't have a market research department but Morsey and a small team started phoning and meeting with as many Ford, Chevy, Dodge and Plymouth owners as possible. They finally made a competitive analysis case for the V-8 and got the six-only decision reversed. "Breech was in the board meeting for two hours and said that he had never been in a meeting like that—not even during his whole time at GM. But he moved that they vote to keep the V-8 in the Fords for '49," said Morsey. Finance argued that it would cost $100 more to make a V-8 than it did a six-cylinder engine and therefore it shouldn't be in the lineup. But Morsey worked with engineering to verify that Ford could make a V-8 for $16 more than a six cylinder and sell it for a $100 premium. And records show that the V-8 was, in fact, a $100 option.

Everyone in the company became cost conscious, cutting anything unnecessary out of the new Ford. "They were as eager as a bunch of shipwrecked sailors," said Crusoe. "This is a nickel-and-dime business all the way through. A dime on a million units is $100,000. We'd practically cut your throat around here for a quarter."

Development of the 1949 Ford

Harold Youngren and Ernie Breech made a visit to the Dearborn Proving Grounds in April of 1947 to see what the new 1949 model sedans (to be introduced in mid-1948) would look like. Youngren, hired by Ford to get a successful post-war model to market in record time, wanted to see the shortcomings so he could consider the changes that would need to be made.

The new model appeared to be too heavy compared to the new, lighter models General Motors was introducing. Commenting on the body style, Youngren said Ford shouldn't put all its hopes on the current Ford design chief, Eugene (Bob) Gregorie. He suggested the design wasn't forward-thinking enough for an all-new model. Youngren was getting deep into the project well before his official hire date of August 1, 1947.

A round-looking design developed by Gregorie as a Ford would ultimately become the new Mercury and what had been designed as the Mercury would then become the new Lincoln. But the new Ford design assignment would be handed to an outside firm for development. Ernie Breech suggested to the Ford operating committee that they let him approach outside design consultant George Walker for fresh vehicle-design ideas, and they consented.

The Forty-Nine Design— Walker or Bourke?

George Walker

George Walker owned his own design studio, George Walker Associates, and had been working primarily for the Nash Motor Company and International Harvester. He had done some component work for Ford before. In his early years, he had played semi-pro football for the Goodyear team in California while getting started in design. Walker had designed roller skates, bikes, breadboxes and chemistry sets before working on Nash car and Kelvinator refrigerator designs for Charles Nash. When Breech approached Walker about doing a design for Ford, he told Walker that Henry II wanted to see him. Walker had never

George W. Walker, a well-known industrial designer, led all Ford design from 1949 to 1954 as an independent consultant. In 1955, he was hired as the first Ford vice president of design. (Photo: Henry Ford Museum and Ford Motor Company)

met Ford and decided it would be an interesting experience, so Breech took him to the Administration Building, the original headquarters located across from the Ford Rotunda in Dearborn. Here he met the young chief for the first time.

In a 1985 George Walker interview with Dave Crippen of the Henry Ford Museum & Greenfield Village, the industrial designer described his first viewing of what the Ford design staff had worked up for the 1949 Ford:

"So, he [Henry Ford] took me over and showed me the car that was supposed to be the 1949 car (Gregorie's design). They were in so much trouble. They had to get out of it and get out of it quick. And, they had to have a car that would be hurried to manufacture and to get dies and everything all set in three months' time. That was unheard of. So, Henry showed me the car. I said, 'Why, that's terrible.' I said, 'You know… ' I was allowed to say it because I wasn't connected with Ford, and I would have, anyhow, and I said, 'It just looks like me stooping over an oven, and it's kinda fat.' " Breech

turned to Henry and asked if he thought this design could be a Mercury instead of the new Ford and Walker supported him on the idea. Henry apparently agreed and asked Walker what he could do to make the new Ford a good selling car. "Well, that's my job," said Walker. "I'll research it to a point, and then I'll do the sketches and all that, but you have to come down with your engineers and look at it every time we call. We won't overdo it."

Walker said he would do the new design for $100,000 and Breech said, "Don't worry about it.

We'll take care of it." But Walker would have to give up two accounts for the Ford project and wasn't all too sure it would be a good business move. Breech said later that he didn't want to talk about it in front of Henry, but that for a five-year program Walker could make $5 million. Although the Ford executive couldn't tell him exactly how he would accomplish this, Walker figured it would be through Ford stock. It was unclear whether Walker ever made his $5 million.

George Walker started to work on the project immediately in the New Center Building in Detroit with a staff of 27 employees, only a few blocks from the GM headquarters building. He told both Ford and Breech that when he called for a review of each stage of the design, the Ford executives would have to come in—pronto. This wasn't a normal three-year program, but a rush to production to beat the competition with what would have to be an exciting vehicle. To further complicate matters, there was still competition between what Walker was designing and what the Gregorie studio within Ford was working on. In the end, Walker's quarter-scale clay model was painted in beige and yellow, and everyone—including Henry and Benson Ford, Ernie Breech, J.R. Davis and Harold Youngren—approved of the design.

According to the Crippen interview with Walker, they then moved on to a full-size clay model. For this review the same board group plus company founder Henry Ford attended. "They all went in there, and I wasn't allowed in there," said Walker. "They all walked around the car, and first of all they showed it to the old man—Mr. Henry Ford—and he took the door handle—it was only stuck in clay—and he threw it on the ground and said, 'That doesn't work.' They laughed, and they laughed, and then when

Robert S. McNamara, the most successful Whiz Kid, was elected president of Ford Motor Company on November 3, 1960. McNamara, seated to left of Chairman Henry Ford II, later resigned to become Secretary of Defense during the Kennedy administration. (Photo: Henry Ford Museum and Ford Motor Company)

they got through, the board came in and okayed it." In a *Ford News* article from 1948, the same story is recounted but has both Clara and Henry viewing the car together. According to the *News* story, Clara broke the door handle and said, "It looked so real."

In a 1957 *Time* magazine article George Walker commented, "There was more significance in the 1949 Ford than the fact that it was different. It had to be. But more than that, it provided the basic concept of our styling since then. Practically all cars at that time had bulging sidelines, particularly around the front and rear fenders. We smoothed those lines out and began the movement toward the integration of the fenders and body."

Robert Bourke

In another Henry Ford Museum/ Crippen interview, industrial designer Robert E. Bourke offered another interesting angle to the story. Bourke said that he and designers Bob Koto (Studebaker)

and Dick Caleal (then recently let go from Chrysler) worked in Caleal's kitchen to build a clay model, hoping to get Dick a job with George Walker. They worked for several days on a quarter-scale clay model, which, according to Bourke, became the base design for the 1949 Ford.

Bourke described the late hours working with Caleal and Koto in Dick's kitchen to put together a clay model. "I had made some sketches for the car. The front end of the car—you can see in the 1949 models and after, I was putting spinners on stuff because of the aircraft. I was a spinner freak." They continued as a team to work up what to them was simply a design that might get their friend a job. Bourke said he just thought it might get Dick a job and then he put it up on a shelf.

Bourke described the look of their design. "The car had vertical taillights instead of the horizontals. They had the faring strip and the horizontals as the way it was built. There was a detail difference as far as the

The mammoth Rouge car manufacturing facility was opened in 1920 and covered 1,200 acres. By 1953 it employed more than 63,000 people and could take raw iron ore in one end and roll a new Ford out the other. The Ford Administration Building and Rotunda are shown in the foreground. (Photo: Henry Ford Museum and Ford Motor Company)

blade that comes off of the spinner in the front. The spinner detail was pretty close on, as was the framing on the top of the spinner." Bourke's design featured the letters F-O-R-D displayed boldly on the sheet metal above the spinner, instead of being part of the chrome. This would be far more costly to assemble. "They had to put the letters on separately, rather than simply stamp them into the header framing."

"If it wasn't for Dick," said Bourke, "it [the '49 Ford design] would never have been done in the first place. It was a real shock to me when that car showed up on the road. It was really a shocker." He said it really wasn't a terrible amount of effort but mostly a few nights of hard work trying to get it finished in time.

Dick Caleal went off to Walker's shop with the clay model in the back seat of his car. When Caleal called Bourke after the Walker visit, he was quite excited saying, "I got the job, Bob." When asked what he thought happened when Walker delivered the design to Ford, Bourke responded, "What did happen is that George Walker sold that particular design to Ford. It's like Loewy sold certain [designs] to Studebaker." Bourke made the point though, that " …if it wasn't for a George Walker and if it wasn't for a Raymond Loewy, there were a lot of things that would have never seen the light of day. But the fact that the '49 Ford design originated in South Bend and one man got a job out of it is enough for me."

Walker, when asked about Bourke's story, said that Dick Caleal said something to him once about having designed the 1949 Ford. According the Crippen interview, Walker was clearly upset with Caleal's comment and characterized him as only doing some clay modeling and blackboard work for his group— that is, interpreting a design line on a blackboard for engineering drawings.

There were obviously a number of people involved with the body design on the 1949 Ford, but it ultimately came out of Walker's design shop. Both Ford and Breech were quite pleased with the final product. It helped to put Ford clearly ahead of both Chevrolet and Chrysler by at least six months.

Launching the Forty-Niner

Production Start-Up

Pilot production of the 1949 Ford, known as the Model B-A, started at the Rouge Plant in early April of 1948, allowing Ford to work out the assembly line "bugs" and start sending completely built-up jobs (completed cars) to other plants as examples to help them get a quick start on production. Because Ford also was introducing the new Mercurys and Lincolns on the heels of the all-new 1948 model truck, Ford now had a totally new lineup of vehicles covering all classes. The B-A model would be the fourth major model change in the company's 45-year history, joining the famed Model T (selling 15 million from 1908–27), the Model A (selling 5 million from 1928–32) and the Model 18 V-8 and the Model B 4-cylinder (selling 12 million from 1932–48). Full production for the B-A started on April 26, 1948, with a grand total of 12 production vehicles rolling out the door. All plants initially built only Tudor (2-door) models, but by May 3, Coupes and Fordors (4-doors) were moving on all lines.

Employee Car Preview

Employees were treated to previews of the finished product as the pilot versions of the new cars rolled off the line. Henry II started a policy of showing his employees new model vehicles before introducing them to the general public. He felt that all employees should be salespersons for their company, telling friends and neighbors about the exciting new products they would soon be seeing. At these "Family Celebrations" employees and their families got a sneak preview of the first models at Ford facilities across the country. The Ford employee newspaper, the *Rouge News*, described the scene:

"The men who make them were given advance showing when some of the new cars were put on display at several locations throughout the Rouge Plant before their public introduction. The new cars were displayed throughout the area, giving employees a preview of the car that revealed a radical change from traditional Ford engineering. Together 150,000 employees and their families attended Family Celebrations at branch plants and parts depots across the nation."

Your Letter Is Your Ticket

Ford employees were encouraged to go home and talk about the vehicles to everyone they knew. In an article in the *Ford Chicago News*, employees were encouraged to bring their families to the Chicago plant on June 13 to see the new cars, entitled *Your Letter Is Your Ticket*.

"*Each Ford Chicago worker will receive a letter from plant manager Simmons inviting him and his family to the family day and plant tour. This letter is important. It must be saved for use as your entrance ticket to Ford Family Day. This is necessary to limit the advance showing to Ford workers and members of their immediate families.*"

June 10 to 15, 1948— Introduction Day

Now that one of the most important vehicles in Ford's history was ready to be released, Henry Ford II decided a fitting debut for the new Ford "Forty-Niner" would be in order. So Ford hired well-known set designer Walter Dorwin Teague to produce an event at New York's Waldorf-Astoria, one of the premier hotels in the nation. The event ran from June 10 to 15, accommodating a sneak preview party for the press and dealers and an unveiling for the general public.

Teague was known for putting together spectacular events going back to the 1933 World's Fair in Chicago. His new creation in the Waldorf included such extravaganzas as a 50-foot merry-go-round, a revolving gold-chassis Ferris wheel, a woodland scene with a 27-foot running stream, a "live" rain storm with a picnic scene, a grove of fully mature trees and a prospector passing out gold nugget buttons with the Ford emblem. The extravaganza covered almost all of the available space in the hotel, including the Grand Ballroom, both foyers, the Basildon Room, the Jade Room and the Astor Gallery.

The Press Reports

The event at the Waldorf-Astoria Hotel was intended to create excitement around the new Fords and garner stories about the event in papers across the country. News reporters from all major U.S. publications were invited to the gala event and filed stories to run during the next several weeks, rarely having anything negative to say about the exotic new vehicle. It was an expensive, but highly successful launch of a vehicle that had to succeed for the company to survive. Following are some of the press comments on the grand and unusual introduction event from some of the major news outlets:

Detroit Free Press, Leo Donovan: *If New York is a criterion, supplying 1949 model Fords to meet public demand will keep the Rouge and other Ford assembly plants [running] for years to come.*

Despite rain, more than 2,000 stood in line outside the 49th Street entrance of the hotel before Mayor William O'Dwyer, of New York, and Ford officially opened the show.

Mrs. Henry Ford, Sr. was one of the estimated 55,000 visitors yesterday at the Ford Motor Company exhibition of 1949 cars at the Waldorf-Astoria Hotel.

She chuckled as she termed the automobile strictly a part "of the man's world" at the turn of the century.

"Now just look down there," she said, pointing to a group of women studying the engine of a Fordor sedan. "Today thousands of women know their own cars as well as they know their sewing machines. They are as familiar with mechanical details and can judge the merits of cars as well as can men."

Los Angeles Times, Bill Henry: After surviving the weekend jam at the Waldorf (70,000 people in one day) you have to come to the conclusion either that this town is full of Californians or else a lot of people are really curious about Henry Ford II's new automobile whether he calls it the "Forty-Niner" or not.

The New Yorker, Talk of the Town (June, 1948): "Ford gave a convincing demonstration at the Waldorf that the 1949 car is lower. The show opened at eleven o'clock, and by twenty minutes past eleven every car on the ballroom floor had dropped out of sight behind the people.

"Our eavesdropping at the show convinced us that the public is well satisfied with the Forty-Niner. America wants a low car. Even more than it wants a low car, it wants a car, and the crowd seemed happy about the Ford. 'Now coming up on your left,' said the announcer, 'is your dream car. The top is raised or lowered with an easy turn of the wrist.' A thousand wrists felt the little, dull pain of despair, and of hope."

The Detroit News, Tony Weitzel: Ex-Chevy Sales Boss Bill Holler trekked up from Florida to catch Ford's New York premiere at the Waldorf…brightened Fordman Frank J. McGinnis' whole week with one-word comment, "Stupendous!"

This color advertisement appeared in the following publications: Saturday Evening Post, Life, Collier's, Country Gentleman, Time, Newsweek, Pathfinder, Farm Journal, and Successful Farming for a total circulation of 21,927,052.

June 18, 1948— Ford Dealers' Public Introduction Day

The Ford Motor Company had carefully built a promotional campaign designed specifically to play on the curiosity of the nation as its dealers took delivery of the new Ford under wraps, with dealers cruising them into garages under car covers in the dark of night so no one could get even a glimpse. Every Ford dealer across the country teased customers with newspaper ads promoting June 18 as the unveiling of one of the most amazing Fords in automotive history. Windows were soaped, cars were in sealed plywood boxes or totally covered with balloons and trucks equipped with speakers drove through crowded city streets announcing that the new cars were now on their way. More than twenty-eight million people filed into Ford showrooms in the first three days at Ford dealerships across the country.

Total attendance and orders taken June 18 - 20 for each region

Region	Attendance	Orders Taken
Southeast	3,281,561	115,377
Central	9,004,926	85,478
Southwest	4,874,716	78,329
Northeast	4,080,573	67,945
Midwest	4,448,111	74,249
West	2,521,521	44,258
Total	**28,211,408**	**465,636**

Dealer Wires Flood Dearborn—June 18, 1948

- "Opened at 4:00 a.m. to clean up cars for display. Visitors started stopping by at that time." —J. B. Harwell, Gurdon, Ark.

- "So many people waiting before opening hour we had to open an hour and ten minutes early." —Transcontinental Garage, Evanston, Wyo.

- "One hundred people waiting to see new car at 6:30 this morning."—J. C. Mahan Motor Co., Knoxville, Tenn.

- "Opened at 6:30 a.m. and our place has been jammed ever since."—W.L. Webster, Schenectady, NY.

- "Crowds were waiting for opening and looking through show windows midnight last night."—Olive-Lilly Motor Co., Grenada, Miss.

- "Traffic is jammed for blocks on El Camino Real due to Tuban's Motors Forty-Niner Ford showing. Do something and do it quick. Suggest increased allotment!" —Les Lutz, Dist. Mgr., Richmond, Calif.

- "Stopped traffic on Monroe Street to extent two policemen sent to handle."—Bob Reese, Toledo, Ohio

The press had been writing about the new Ford since the preview in New York. This was, of course, exactly what Ford's public relations team had hoped for. They got an initial burst of stories in the first few days and then a steady flow of stories in the weekly and monthly magazines during the first weeks the cars were in the showrooms.

- "The new car was certainly as advertised, Ford's most radical facelifting since the Model A. It was definitely modern and definitely slinky." *Newsweek*, June 14

- "Now in one sweeping model change his 30-year-old grandson/successor Henry Ford II has brought the Ford not merely even with Chevrolet and Plymouth but out in front of them." *Life*, June 14

- "Even Ford's Model A, which supplanted the famed old Model T that virtually placed America on wheels, did not click as enthusiastically as did the 1949 cars." Leon J. Pinkson, *San Francisco Chronicle*

- "Whether people will prefer to swoon, gaze, or stare unbelievingly at the new Ford cannot be said, but its remarkable changes will throw many for a loop. Eye doctors are expecting a rush business after today, and Ford dealers are expecting an even greater rush." Patti McGee, *Wetumka* (Okla.) *Gazette*

▶

Ford brothers (left to right) William Clay, Benson and Henry posed in a public relations photo to promote the company's millionth 1949 Ford. (Photo: Henry Ford Museum and Ford Motor Company)

FORD

The Year 1949

This Tudor model is similar to the Ford driven by Robert Mitchum in the movie Thunder Road. *They were light, nimble and had plenty of power with the V-8 torque.*

Showing a Profit

Nineteen forty-nine was the first real breath of fresh air the Ford Motor Company experienced in a long time. Its new car line had been launched in mid-1948, so the company had a six-month lead on Chevrolet in which to close the gap on sales as well as profits. Profits were up substantially, with net income at 7.8 percent of sales, an increase of 4.7 percent over 1948. Ford had been making heavy investments in new facilities and equipment to the tune of $270 million in the previous four years, gambling that its future products would pay off.

The Rouge Plant was already producing 750 completed Ford and Mercury vehicles in an eight-hour shift by April, 1948. But Ford suffered one union work stoppage during May, along with continuing material shortages, which held back production.

Still, the company ran a record 1,322,424 cars and trucks out the door, up from just over one million in 1948.

With the increase in passenger car production, Ford output was up 26 percent. If you added Lincoln and Mercury to the totals, it was up 44 percent. Truck production on the other hand declined in 1949 by more than 50,000 units. Ford had 42 percent of the total car and truck market in 1930 but had dropped to about 19 percent in 1948. By 1949 the company was back up to a 21 percent share and the future was looking good.

In short, the company had most of its management reorganization in place, a complete lineup of new cars and trucks, new facilities, better engineering leadership and refined manufacturing processes. There was still plenty to do but the new management had made substantial headway toward a renaissance of Ford Motor Company.

Ford had hired key GM executives to revamp the company and shamelessly copied the "General's" business management style. And why not? They saw this as the only way to leapfrog back to the top of a highly competitive automotive industry. Ford could not afford to let the golden opportunity of sales in the post-war years slip by. The economy was robust and it was just what Ford needed to get back in the ball game. Henry Ford II finally had it all moving in the right direction but needed to put the last big piece of the decentralization puzzle in place.

		Sales Progress 1946-49		
Year	Passenger Cars	Trucks	Buses	Total
1946	457,368	198,767	2,513	**658,648**
1947	755,552	247,832	2,256	**1,005,640**
1948	747,467	301,791	363	**1,049,621**
1949	1,077,641	244,613	170	**1,322,424**

Birth of Ford Division— February 11, 1949

Ernie Breech and Henry Ford II were getting along famously, constantly thinking along the same lines with the goal of reorganizing Ford Motor Company and turning a good profit. Breech and Ford talked over lunch, walked into each other's office unannounced and communicated constantly to move their ideas ahead quickly.

Although no project of this magnitude is ever complete, by 1949 they both felt that they had accomplished their primary goals and had much of the reorganization in place. They now had a full organizational chart flowing from their names at the top on down to the divisional heads of all the major areas of concern. There was a good master plan and specific goals to be met by each division leader.

In 1945, the Lincoln and Mercury lines and all the business parts related with their assembly and sales were organized into a Lincoln-Mercury Division. This was a first step in the decentralization plan that Breech and Ford had opted for. The International Division was formed in 1946 and staff organizations such as advertising, manufacturing, purchasing, finance and public relations were in place by the end of that year. The office of the general counsel (legal section) was formed in 1947.

Breech, still following the example of GM's Alfred Sloan, next moved to put a major piece of the puzzle in place by forming a division dedicated wholly to the Ford model product, the heart of the company's potential profits. L.D. Crusoe, one of Breech's two key men, was appointed as the first head of Ford Division. The division was officially signed off by the board on February 11 and announced to the public on February 15, 1949. This would bring accountability to each arm of the business, highlighting how efficiently or inefficiently it was being run. Everything from cost to quality would be affected.

One thing that led to the decision to bring assembly, sales, advertising, purchasing, finance and service under one roof for the Ford model products was the apparent high level of minor defects in the 1949 Ford, running into the thousands. Crusoe had promised the dealers that the problems would be fixed in the 1950 model, but one inherent defect was the poor body fit that allowed moisture and dust to enter the interior.

The theory was that if the complete process of designing, building, selling and servicing a new car could be brought under one operation, it would be far easier to figure out where any particular problem lay. It would also be much easier to correct it and to keep it from happening again. The reorganization also helped identify which operations were profitable and which ones were dragging the company down. So Ford Division began under the firm hand of L. D. Crusoe with its first challenge to pass Chevrolet in sales. The unofficial slogan became, "Beat Chevrolet!"

Timeline
- British author George Orwell publishes the futuristic novel *1984*
- Rodgers and Hammerstein's musical, *South Pacific*, debuts on Broadway in New York City
- The Soviet Union detonates its first atomic bomb
- The *Lone Ranger* debuts on TV
- Movie of the year: *All the King's Men*
- Grand jury indicts Preston Tucker and associates

With the Ford Division complete by 1949, Henry II and Breech had the organization fully in place and the Lincoln-Mercury, Ford and International Divisions were all considered profit centers.

Products

The Forty-Niner

Ford spent more than $37.4 million in tools, dies, jigs and fixtures to develop and produce the new line of Ford cars and tens of millions more on design, engineering and facilities. The estimated total cost to bring the 1949 Ford to market was more than $118 million, a mammoth figure for 1949. Getting the car in front of customers quickly— ahead of new Chevrolet and Plymouth models—was of utmost importance.

The 1949 Ford Deluxe was the style leader in the low-priced field. By bringing the new model to market six months ahead of Chevrolet's and Plymouth's post-war models, Ford quickly jumped into second place for sales. (Photo: Henry Ford Museum and Ford Motor Company)

Ford leapt past the entire low-priced field with the new post-war models. It now had plenty of room, extra passenger and luggage space and was mechanically much advanced over anything on the road. The profile of the convertible was graceful with its rounded fenders and neat, clean trim.

The driving position of the new Ford was far superior to previous models with much better vision over the new, rounded hood line. The optional push-button radio and clock were but a glance away from the driver in the center of the dash.

Rear seating was wonderful for a convertible with the width easily accommodating three passengers. A combination of leather and Bedford cord upholstery came standard with the convertible.

Luggage space was nearly twice that of the 1948 model Fords, holding 19 cubic feet.

Spotlights were optional and the outside driver's mirror was a popular add-on, though it wouldn't become standard equipment for many years.

Convertibles came standard with a 239 cubic-inch flathead V-8 engine producing 100 horsepower, only five more than the six-cylinder. Both engines used Holley carburetors and had a 6.8:1 compression ratio, allowing them to run on regular fuel.

The convertible model came, like the other models, without fender skirts and many buyers bought the factory optional ribbed skirts shown here.

This Sportsman model was never produced. By the time Ford was ready to introduce the new vehicles, the company was trying to get rid of complicated models and chose to only add wood to the wagons. Ford already knew the wood-clad models were low volume and low profit and Ford was focusing on making money—not losing it. (Photo: Henry Ford Museum and Ford Motor Company)

The estimates of how long the process took vary, but a 1948 *Popular Science* article says it was 14 months from the drafting board to final design approval. Ford was using an 18-month figure inside the company and vowed to never again try doing a car so quickly. The defect rate was too high a price to pay even though the car was considered a success in the marketplace.

The push was intended to get the new Ford to dealers ahead of Chevrolet and Plymouth. It was first thought that Chevy might have its model out by early 1948 but the model actually made it to market almost a year later, putting Ford several months ahead of Chevy with its June introduction.

Ford objectives for the new model included an exciting, different body design, all-new engineering and more interior room and comfort. It really had only two things in common with the 1948 models. The Forty-Niner shared the earlier models' 114-inch wheelbase, although it used a totally new ladder-type frame, and the flathead, or L-head, V-8, which had a number of improvements. Everything else was completely new.

Interior

The fabrics in the '49 interiors were much more daring and colorful than in the past. The new cloth on the seats consisted of tweeds, broadcloths and mohair. This, along with more exterior colors and numerous optional accessories, gave the post-war customer some wonderful ways to spend his or her money, leaving the boring, gray colors of the war behind. After several years of war rationing and doing without, buyers wanted something other than a black car with a drab-looking interior, so Ford gave it to them. The addition of choices and style kept buyers coming even when the quality was not great.

Interior room and trunk space was dramatically improved over the old 1948 design. The new Ford had a lower profile with smooth lines. Trunk space increased by 57 percent, to 19 cubic feet. And the trunk was much more usable for storing cargo due to the '49-model's squared-off rear end. The Forty-Niner's wheelbase remained the same as the '48's, but with the engine now forward by five inches, there was more leg space. This also allowed designers

to include seats that ran the full width of the vehicle instead of being wedged between the wheelwells, giving six inches more width for the front seat and eight inches more for the rear. Passengers were no longer crowded and the vehicle truly seated six adults comfortably. A good part of the newfound width came from a wider body, now flush with the outer edges of the fenders. Interior width was no longer restricted to the distance between the running boards. Space planning was far superior to any other vehicles of the time.

The air in Ford's new interior was controlled with either a standard high-speed fan and heater system or the optional Magic Air temperature control. Magic Air provided the driver with control of airflow volume and temperature and came equipped with a 2-speed fan. The new heating and ventilation system received air from large ducts located behind the grille that provided far better air circulation than before. Ford claimed that the large intake of air provided more pressure in the interior, helping to reduce dust and moisture seepage and keeping interior glass from fogging. But many reports from owners said that dust and water leakage was a common problem in the Forty-Niner, an inherent design flaw due to the poor-fitting cowl and body panels. This would also imply that Magic Air didn't provide much in the way of pressurization.

The dust and moisture problem was recognized early on and some interim fixes were tried at the assembly plants while engineering looked at longer-term corrections. At 18 years of age, Del Peterson went to work at the Twin Cities Assembly Plant in Minnesota. "There were a lot of quality problems with the '49 Ford," Peterson recalled. "One of the jobs I had in 1950 was to put a very heavy asphalt deadener in all the cars that were coming down the line prior to being painted. That had to do with the well-acknowledged problem of leaking dust and moisture and also excessive noise. They were trying to do what they could to solve the problems by putting this thick mastic stuff in the trunks and floor pans." The problems were never completely solved in the 1949 to 1951 models, but

merely patched. In the Nevins and Hill book, *Ford: Decline and Rebirth*, L. D. Crusoe told his sales managers that they were going to have to live with the shortcomings of the old design until the '52 came to market."

On the evening of December 15, 1948, a fire broke out at the Dearborn Assembly Plant, causing approximately $450,000 worth of damage. Production of the Ford models wasn't resumed until December 21, and the Mercury line wasn't started again until January 3, 1949. While making repairs to the fire-damaged assembly line, many improvements were implemented as part of the rebuild to speed up daily production and increase quality. The schedules at both the St. Louis and the Metuchen, New Jersey, plants were stepped up to help replace some of the lost production.

Henry Ford II, in an open letter to the employees, said, "During the past two years we have gone to a lot of trouble here at Ford to find out what our employees thought of us. Sometimes the results were not too flattering." But he went on to

compliment the Dearborn plant workers on quickly pitching in when the fire broke out to push unfinished cars off the line and helping in many other ways. "Without their help there would have been additional property damage and greater loss of employment and production." He went on to say that because he couldn't get to all the employees in the various buildings to thank them, he would do so in an open letter in the *Rouge News* employee paper. Ford made a point of developing good relations with his employees, realizing early

1949 Model Car Pricing		
	Six-cylinder	V-8
Business Coupe	$1236	$1318
Tudor Sedan	$1323	$1393
Fordor Sedan	$1368	$1438
Club Coupe	$1313	$1415
Ford Custom line		
Tudor Sedan	$1405	$1480
Fordor Sedan	$1450	$1525
Club Coupe	$1405	$1485
Convertible	$1759	$1820
Station Wagon	$1980	$2118

Ford used a series of cartoon advertising during the 1949–59 period. This series featured Al Esper, Ford's chief test driver, talking to "Wally." Young Wally was obviously impressed with the features on the new Forty-Niner.

on that he needed a positive team of workers to produce cars—in both volume and quality. He used his employee newspapers across the country effectively as a method of communication especially the *Rouge News*.

New design

The 1949 body design was the first for Ford to offer smooth, slab sides, incorporating the fenders and the body. Although the new design had smooth, rounded edges, it also had a much more practical shape for carrying people and luggage. With the trunk featuring a more squared-off design instead of the old sloping shape, it could carry suitcases and boxes much more efficiently.

Only two model lines were offered—the Ford and the Ford Custom lines. Both were available in Tudor and Fordor models and a Club Coupe. The Tudor and Fordor were promotional names for 2-door and 4-door sedans Ford adopted for its Model T sedans in 1924 and brought back for the new models. The Convertible and Wagon series were offered only in the Custom line and were the only models to continue using an X-style frame. This was to ensure necessary rigidity.

The '49 wagon was the first of the Fords to use all-steel construction, providing a stiffer body and a tighter, squeak-free ride. Prior to the 1949 wagons, "woodies" with a wood frame were produced at the Ford Iron Mountain facility in northern Michigan.

Engineering Changes

The new Ford was originally code-named X-2900, designating it as experimental with a targeted weight of 2,900 pounds. The final version came in at 3,150 pounds, going over the target but still 220 pounds less than the '48 model. Keeping it lighter would give the customer a better handling and performing vehicle with improved mileage. Losing the extra weight was like finding more horsepower and miles per gallon almost for free, making it peppier and more agile compared to the older models.

Engines

Fuel economy, according to Ford, was increased by 10 percent in both the six-cylinder and the V-8. Of course, the earlier Fords were not a model of efficiency and improving them wasn't much of a challenge. A new intake manifold provided better fuel distribution. With the optional overdrive manual transmission, economy

This 1949 Ford print ad boasted that Ford was the "one and only new car in its field." In many ads, Ford stated that the new model was "the car of the year," although this had nothing to do with an award.

In its second year, the 1949 F-1 pickups were still selling well and bringing the Ford truck owners into the decade of the 1950s. The new cabs were a major step forward in providing the working class with more comfort while they worked.

could be improved up to 25 percent.

The new overdrive transmission was a popular item, and many customers couldn't get it at the time of purchase. The overdrive typically added two miles per gallon to the mileage figures. At 2,306 revolutions per minute (rpm), a car without overdrive would be traveling 50 miles per hour while the one with the new overdrive would be running 65 miles per hour. Another side benefit of the overdrive gear was less engine wear over the life of the car.

With a redesigned cooling system, the engine ran cooler by 12F (7 degrees Celsius). The new "equal-flow" system moved water directly to the rear of the block, then up to the cylinder head(s) and back to the radiator. The flathead design in both engines had been plagued with "hot spots" in previous years but this cooling

system appeared to take care of the problem, moving the water from the bottom of the block and out through the top. V-8 models used a larger water pump to cool the engine. Ford expected lower warranty costs, but as the warranties were only 90 days or 4,000 miles, this wasn't a big consideration. They were more interested in actually keeping the customer happy with the improvements.

The engine was now set on rubber mounts to lessen vibration. Ford redesigned the combustion chambers and improved the crankcase ventilation system in the V-8. Better-insulated spark plug wires were added to prevent cross-firing between plugs. These small improvements were long overdue and probably more valuable to the customer than anything else that might have been done.

The 226 cubic-inch six-

cylinder flathead produced 95 horsepower at 3,300 rpm and the 239 cubic-inch V-8 was rated at 100 horsepower at 3,600 rpm. Both had a 6.8 to 1 compression ratio, allowing them to run on almost any kind of fuel. Although the Ford V-8 only had a 5-horsepower advantage over the six, the V-8 provided more torque for better takeoff and a great sound. It was still the only V-8 offered in the low-price field.

F-series trucks

The 1949 F-1 pickup models were much the same as the previous year's trucks. The available engines were the standard 95-horsepower Rouge 226 six-cylinder, available in F-1 through F-6 models, and the Rouge 239 flathead V-8 with 100 horses. The F-1 through F-3 series trucks had a new, optional heavy-duty 3-speed transmission for the 1949 season,

This illustrated print ad highlighted more directly the new brag points of the '49 Ford. It showed the two engine choices, Hydra-Coil suspension, luggage compartment with 57 percent more space, rigid Life Guard body and new flight panel dash.

but little else changed because the trucks had been introduced as all-new only a year before and the company was directing most of its resources toward the Forty-Niner automobile.

The pickup bed had hardwood sub-floors, sandwiched between a metal outer surface with stamped metal runners on the top surface. Forty-nine inches wide, the bed could easily hold a standard 4-foot wide sheet of plywood and was long enough to carry a 7-foot door. The sidewalls of the bed still had raised stampings for rigidity. The top edges of the bed sides had rolled edges that, according to the dealer brochures, strengthened the body and offered a better sliding surface for objects loaded from the side.

Crushing parts

Del Peterson described an odd job during his first summer at the Twin Cities plant: "I had one interesting job the first summer I was at Ford. The plants had what they called a 'service dock' that shipped parts to the dealers direct from the plant. That summer they had gone through their inventory and decided what old or slow-moving parts they wanted to get rid of. Before they sent these parts to the scrap yard, they had to be destroyed to the point they couldn't be resold. I remember spending several days with hammers and presses smashing up brand-new old-stock parts. This included everything from piston rings, cold trim, hub caps, whatever they felt they had an excess of in inventory." Peterson said even at that time it seemed ridiculous to be doing this, but

now, he really cringes to think about all the parts they destroyed.

Suspension

One major improvement in the new Ford was the suspension. The fully independent front suspension provided better ride and handling characteristics and flatter cornering. It was far superior on bumpy roads, but because this was Ford's first independent front suspension, they learned soon enough that proper travel and shock valving would be a concern. The new models tended to bottom out under sharp dips and potholes in the road, placing a sound jolt through the frame to the passengers. New "hydra-coil" springs replaced the Ford traditional transverse springs for a much smoother and more stable ride with what was described as "airplane-type shock absorbers." On the 1949–51 models, the shock absorbers looked the same and the specifications were similar, but the feel of the vehicles were quite different. "The '49 had an overall loose feel," according to Del Peterson. "You would go over bumps and the car would shake. It just felt kind of floppy, although nothing ever really went wrong with it—it was a good car. The '50 model just seemed to feel more secure. And the '51 was even tighter."

For the Forty-Niner, the driveshaft tunnel height was decreased by adapting a Hotchkiss drive system and a hypoid rear axle. These changes kept road noise transmitted to the interior to a minimum. It also reduced the size of the large driveshaft tunnel under the feet of the center passenger. It was still there, but was less obtrusive.

Safety

Not much was being done in the area of safety by any of the manufacturers during the early 1950s, but Ford considered the strengthening of the chassis and stiffening of the body (59 percent more rigid than the older models) a safety advantage and advertised it as such. The overall lower ride height (4 inches lower) provided a lower center of gravity for better handling and less likelihood of rolling over. Ford also pointed out that with almost 20 square feet of glass window space, the driver had better visibility as well.

One safety bragging point Ford claimed for its new station wagon was selling only a 2-door model with extra-large doors: "Careless or playful children cannot accidentally lean against or bump the door handles to open the doors while the car is in motion." Never mind that Ford reintroduced a 4-door model again in 1952 with an "all steel, 4-door modern design body."

The real reason for only selling the 2-door model was more likely a limited budget with which to bring these cars to market quickly.

Advertising and Promotion

The advertising theme of 1949 was, "There could be a Ford in your future." One ad said, "It'll light a bonfire in your heart but it won't burn a hole in your pocketbook!" Ford wanted to deliver the message that you could spend more money but you couldn't get a better product. *Mechanix Illustrated* writer Tom McCahill supported this theory in an article, asking the reader, "Why have expensive cars then, you ask?" He went on to suggest the only reasons were snob appeal, better ride, more power and usually better performance. "From there on in you are forced to act like a ward-heeler the day before election to think up any other legitimate reasons [for buying a more costly car]." This too was Ford's marketing strategy, giving customers more for their money. Large cars weren't safer, were usually harder to handle, and they didn't last any longer.

Ford often used percentages in their advertising and dealer materials to dramatize just how different the new cars were compared to the earlier models. This list was taken from just one brochure:

- 59% more rigid Life Guard body
- 35% less pedal pressure on the new King Size brakes
- 10% more fuel economy
- 25% more fuel economy with the new overdrive option
- 57% more luggage space
- 88% more visibility with the new rear window
- 12% more glass area

Ford often used advertising to focus on its people, corporate philosophy and quality to give potential customers a better image of the company. In the past Ford had been known more as a producer of affordable but low-quality vehicles.

A *Life* magazine advertisement covering two facing pages described "Ford ace test driver" Roy Bannister as he road-tested a '49 model equipped with "new secret parts and features developed by Ford research."

The Michigan State Police liked using flathead Ford V-8s because of their great high performance. (Photo: Henry Ford Museum and Ford Motor Company)

The F-6 model Ford trucks were capable of hauling anything from a new Ford tractor to heavy loads of lumber.

In this photo spread, Roy drives from Michigan to the Arizona desert to first do testing in the 120-degree heat to check for vapor lock and other engine-related problems. The car was described as a '49 body with a combination of 1950–51 running gear underneath. With a total of more than 26,000 miles on the odometer for his trip, Roy had covered the deserts, mountains and high-speed testing in various terrain. The photo essay wraps up with Roy at home standing by his Ford. "A wonderful trip," says Roy to his wife, Bette Mae, and daughter, Barbara, as he brings back 35 pages of notes taken on his adventure.

These ads were designed to mold Ford's reputation as a producer of quality, affordable vehicles that did not neglect the human factor. Ford often included its employees in advertising, delivering the message that the people who design Ford vehicles are just like you and me. The tag line said, "It's part of the Ford way of doing business…making the best possible products in the best possible way…to benefit producer, consumer and the nation as a whole."

The new Fords, even with their low initial quality, had a high-style look and now were on their way to success. The management team saw this success in the late 1940s as a temporary means of bringing profits back into the company, but realized that they had much work to do before the 1950 models started rolling off the lines.

▶

The Country Squire was marketed as a vehicle for country clubs, upscale hotels and a high-class business car. (Photo: Henry Ford Museum and Ford Motor Company)

FORD

The Year 1950

The Custom Deluxe Club Coupe was the sporty hardtop model offered by Ford in 1950. The Coupe could be had with a six-cylinder or a V-8 and was a favorite of lead-footing drivers. Club Coupe pricing started at $1485.

Production of the 1950 passenger cars began in early November, 1949, and the public received its first viewing in late November. The cars appeared to be nearly identical to the Forty-Niner models but in fact were much improved. Dust and water stopped coming through cracks in the body, steering was better and the new models had a much tighter feel overall.

For the first half of 1950, Ford Motor Company was rolling cars out the plant doors with plenty of parts, a healthy labor force and lots of customers. The company was well organized, making a good profit, had a full lineup of excellent cars and trucks the public wanted and was investing the profits back into new facilities for the future. But on June 24, the North Koreans moved more than 60,000 troops into South Korea and President Truman quickly arranged to send in American soldiers to assist the South. By early August, both Ford and GM were organizing defense arms of their companies to prepare to help the U.S. government.

As Ford prepared to do its part in the national effort, the government also set out to limit the production of vehicles by each manufacturer. This was done to start conserving many precious resources the government would need as the manufacturers prepared for heavy military production. By limiting its production, the company's profits were limited as well. Ford, while still working on becoming more efficient in its design and production methods, had to post lower profits during this period. In 1950 Ford posted a profit of $259 million. In 1951, profits dropped to $126 million, and in 1952, totals would sink to $116 million.

Even during these times of limited production, Ford Division vehicles managed to improve market share, from 16.4 percent in 1949 to 17.8 percent in 1950. Ford Motor Company as a whole moved up from a 21.2 percent share in '49 to 23.8 percent in 1950. Fueling the record industry production of more than six million cars was the buying public's fear of another war rationing program similar to that imposed during World War II. Apparently the public moved quickly to get what new cars they could find. This, plus a government-forced production cutback, did cause a temporary shortage of vehicles. Fortunately production was only partially slowed, unlike World War II, when it stopped completely.

Products

The company made many minor changes to the '50 Ford, primarily to correct a number of the deficiencies in the 1949 model. The visual clues that it was a '50 model came from a slightly different hood ornament, a new Ford crest, new parking lights and a fuel-filler door instead of an external gas cap. But hidden from the eye were improvements to body fit, rubber seals around the windshield and rear window, stronger door latches and a tighter, better handling suspension. The interior featured a reshaped horn ring, a repositioned hand brake and a double-walled glove box with a better designed hinge. Added together, these and other changes to the 1950 models became one of the advertising themes of this year: "50 ways new for '50!"

Deluxe

With introduction of the Custom Deluxe series, the Deluxe was now the low-line vehicle. The Ford Deluxe models included the Fordor, Tudor and Business Coupe. All came standard with dual windshield wipers, twin horns, one sun visor, foam rubber padded front seats, an interior light on the left B-pillar and a glove box in the dash panel. Starting prices for a six-cylinder Deluxe were $1,236 and $1,318 with a V-8.

Custom Deluxe

A buyer who moved up to the Custom Deluxe series enjoyed plenty of extra trim and comfort items. This top-line series carried body styles in Fordor, Tudor, Club Coupe, Business Coupe, Station Wagon or Convertible. The interior included dual sun visors, a locking glove box, an electric clock (extra cost in sedans and coupes), a cigar lighter and assist straps for aiding rear passengers on exit in coupes.

Deluxe series came standard with 16-inch wheels, while the Custom Deluxe came with 15-inch rims and 6.70x15 4-ply tires. White sidewalls were optional on all models. All series were available with either the six-cylinder or V-8 engine, overdrive, hydraulic brakes, semi-floating hypoid differential and a worm-and-roller steering gear.

Crestliner

Ford introduced the Crestliner, a two-tone steel-top sports sedan, in July of 1950 to compete with Chevrolet's new Bel Air Model.

The Bel Air was designed to look like a hardtop convertible and Ford didn't yet have anything to compete, so they needed a quick fix to hold them over until the all-new Victoria could be brought to market six months later.

Timeline
- The United States goes to war in Korea—material shortages affect auto production
- U.S. Senator Joseph McCarthy begins his inquiry into un-American activities
- NBC's *Hit Parade, You Bet Your Life,* starring Groucho Marx, and *The Adventures of Superman* debut on television
- Tucker and associates found not guilty
- U.S. car and truck production soars to an unheard-of eight million units for the year
- Henry Ford's wife, Clara Ford, dies
- Sears introduces the Allstate, a car built by Kaiser-Frazer to be sold through its catalog
- Movie of the year: *All About Eve*

Although optional, many new Fords were equipped with white wall tires as the craze caught on. Ford also strengthened the body at 13 critical points and promoted it as a "Life Guard" body.

The "Fashion Car" for 1950 had a new Ford crest that was mounted on both the hood, just below the restyled ornament, and on the rear deck. The crest wasn't actually a family crest, but rather a Ford-created medallion to reflect a heritage feel about their vehicles.

Ford was still using a six-volt electric system. Holley carburetors were used on both the six-cylinder and V-8 Ford engines.

This Custom Deluxe Club Coupe in Coronation red was only one of eleven new colors offered to potential buyers. Part of the Ford marketing strategy was to add fresh colors and interiors to match the forward looking body design.

The newly developed Ford crest was on the hood and rear deck of all Ford models.

Seats in the '50 models featured new springs and sponge rubber cushions that better held their shape – a problem with the Forty-Niner. Magic Air had a higher speed fan to provide a 25 percent increase in air flow and the glove box was now a double walled construction with an improved hinge.

Ford's new hood ornament was a light, airy looking piece that went along with the rest of the smooth hood and fender styling.

This 1950 Ford public relations photo was trying to suggest that the Country Squire wagon was cool for a guy to drive. It actually sold in relatively low numbers, was difficult to maintain and had low resale value. (Photo: Henry Ford Museum and Ford Motor Company)

The Crestliner was a standard Club Coupe body with a rather odd-looking two-tone color scheme. The top was a black "basket weave" vinyl and on the sides of each front fender and stretching across the door just into the rear panel was a large black rounded section. The rest of the body came in either Coronation red or Sportsman's green. The Crestliner was priced at $1,785 FOB Detroit. This was $70 more than a Fordor and $225 less than a convertible. Gold-colored die-cast Crestliner emblems were mounted on each fender. This strange combination of colors and chrome was an obvious attempt at a quick response to the Bel Air, and despite all the effort, the model never sold well.

Country Squire Station Wagon

Ford's wagon for 1950 was initially called the Custom Deluxe V-8 Station Wagon and later in production was re-introduced as the Country Squire.

Before the 1949 model all-steel wagons, the bodies were of wood construction, screwed and glued together at the Iron Mountain, Michigan, plant. Ford had pioneered the woody-style station wagon with the Model A in 1929 and the Iron Mountain plant was still producing the steel-bodied variations for the 1949 to 1951 models. A big problem with the pre-1949 models was that after a very short period of ownership, the bodies began squeaking and rattling, and resale value started dropping fast. The woody wagons were much sought-after for use

1950 Model Car Pricing		
	Six-cylinder	V-8
Ford Deluxe		
Business Coupe	$1236	$1318
Tudor Sedan	$1323	$1393
Fordor Sedan	$1368	$1438
Ford Custom Deluxe		
Tudor Sedan	$1405	$1480
Fordor Sedan	$1450	$1525
Club Coupe	$1405	$1485
Convertible Club Coupe		$1820
Ford Crestliner V-8*		$1595
Country Squire Wagon**	$1895	$1970

*Crestliner was a late introduction— July 1950

**Also called Custom Deluxe V-8 Station Wagon early in production

at hotels, country clubs and even in movies, but maintaining or rebuilding them was a costly nightmare.

Ford wagons for 1950 were a continuation of the welded all-steel construction started in 1949. As in 1949, wagons were offered only in a 2-door body style with steel body panels. The wood look continued with exterior panels of real mahogany and birch or maple framing applied to the steel body. The center seat would fold down and the rear seat was easily removed without use of tools. This 8-seat format was a forerunner of today's minivans and sport-utility vehicles.

The 1949 to 1951 model station wagon bodies were shipped directly from Ford's Iron Mountain facility, where the wooden trim and panels were completely prepared—from cutting the trees to laminating the wood and attaching it to the metal body panels. This same facility had been making wooden-bodied wagons since 1929, and also gliders during World War II. The bodies were shipped to assembly sites almost complete, loaded vertically with the tail end up in the air. They were completely painted, the exterior wood trim was in place, and the instrument panels installed. They were then unloaded at the plant and placed on the assembly line for the rest of the assembly process.

The wooden-clad wagons were to be short-lived because they were the most costly models to produce, had the lowest production volume and the lowest resale value of the Ford lineup. By 1952, Ford would move away from real wood on the wagons due to its impracticality, looking for more quality and durability for the customer— especially because Chevy and Plymouth were outselling Ford with their all-steel models. The wood panels were difficult to replace after the weather took its

toll and dealers soon tired of carrying the replacement panels.

Engineering and Other Changes

The more serious changes were in the hidden form of a much improved front suspension with more travel, firmer front seat cushions to deter sag, a stronger frame, rotary door locks, a new deck-lid latch and better standard interior ventilation with a high-speed fan.

The flathead V-8 for 1950 underwent several changes that

actually improved it into one of its best years. It had major improvements in 1933, correcting many serious shortcomings from its introduction a year earlier, but it had few other changes until Harold Youngren came into the picture in the late 1940s.

A new 3-blade fan was utilized to cut down noise under the hood. The camshaft timing gear was now a laminated composition material, replacing the aluminum 1949 gear for quieter operation. Also reducing noise was a new camshaft with longer opening and closing ramps to quiet cacophonous tappets.

With available V-8 power, Ford had a key advantage over Chevy and Plymouth, which only came with six-cylinder engines.

The Ford F-1 pickups for 1950 didn't change anything the naked eye could see, but did have minor improvements over the 1948–49 models. The 1950 model was started by turning the key in the ignition switch to the right and then pushing the starter button. Ford trucks set an all-time sales record of 358,000 trucks, 130,00 higher than in 1949.

The 1950 Crestliner was an attempt to respond quickly to Chevrolet's sporty, new Bel Air model. The Crestliner was in low demand and only a hold-over until the new Victoria model came out a few months later. (Photo: Henry Ford Museum and Ford Motor Company)

Wheels on the Deluxe models were 16-inch diameter and on the Custom Deluxe, 15-inches with wider 6.70 inch width 4-ply tires. Overdrive was available with either the manual or Fordomatic transmissions.

The 1950 flathead V-8 now used Nelson autothermic pistons to help eliminate piston slap. The aluminum pistons used a steel expansion-control strut cast into them to prevent shrinkage in cold operating temperatures and swelling in extreme heat.

The flathead V-8 had a reputation for using oil, so Ford engineers added rubber seal rings on the intake valve guides to prevent oil from running down the valve stems and into the combustion chambers. Also aiding durability was an oil squirt hole in each connecting rod to help lubricate the cylinder walls during a cold start. Said Youngren about this engineering update, "They are the quietest and smoothest running engines we have ever produced."

A faster heater fan motor in the new models increased airflow by 25 percent. Door-jamb switches now controlled the pillar-mounted lights automatically.

Accessories

Ford had a history of offering many "dealer-installed" accessories to the customer. This helped dealer profits, and reduced complexity for Ford manufacturing and offered the customer a wide array of add-on items to individualize his vehicles—even after purchase.

Some of the more popular accessories were:

- **Custom radio.** "The Ford Custom radio for '50 is unsurpassed in beauty of tone and all-around performance," said one Ford brochure. "You have only to hear its rich, full voice to appreciate the quality of workmanship built in." This model had a seven-tube super heterodyne receiver with three dual-purpose tubes.
- **Deluxe radio.** This top-of-the-line Ford radio option was a five-tube model with pushbutton tuning for five stations. It also came with a "superior 6 x 9-inch speaker" and had "crystal-clear reception—engineered to match the acoustics of the '50 Ford."
- **Spotlights.** Spotlights were a popular item, especially during the late 1940s and the 1950s. They typically were used more for looks than practicality. "It's well-nigh indispensable when looking for road signs or street numbers at night. You can rely on its powerful beam to spot bad curves and dangerous obstacles along the road," said one Ford brochure.

Convertibles came with a hydraulic powered top controlled with a T-handle on the dash. The top folded neatly behind the rear seat and came with a snap-on cover to give it a clean appearance. The '50 Convertible sold for $1820.

Part of the improvement package for the second year of the new series was rubber seals and moldings on the windshield and back window to reduce water leaks.

Twisting the pistol grip directed the light to the target spot. It had a built-in on/off switch in the handle.

- **Road lamps.** Chrome-plated driving lights could be mounted on the front bumper for bad driving conditions.
- **Backup lamps.** Optional backup lights were mounted on the body below the tail lamps and just outside of the vertical bumper guards. They came on when the gear lever was directed into reverse. These could be bought and installed in pairs or for the left side only.

A Year of Growth

Nineteen-fifty was a year of growth and profit for Ford, and a year of learning. It had been the most successful year in Ford Motor Company history, posting a net income of $259 million, even though most of the profits and production were taken during the first half of the year. When the Korean War set in, many restrictions were put in place. In 1947, Ford had a net income of only $2,000, but by 1950 production and profits were up 44 percent over 1949. The industry average was up only 28 percent. This turnaround could be directly attributed to Henry Ford II and Ernie Breech. They had built a new team and charged ahead, cutting costs while restructuring the way Ford did its business. Now they were reaping the spoils of the manufacturing wars. General Motors was still far ahead, but Ford was healthy and moving up fast.

Ford had upgraded, fixed and patched the second year of the Forty-Niner series into a much better product to help achieve these increased sales and profits. The car was a long way from being an engineering marvel, but it ran great, handled well and was affordable for the buying public. In the low-price range of vehicles available to the American market, Ford was now considered a great value. It was far superior to the '49 version, it was the only car in its field that had a V-8 and the body style was cutting edge for the day.

Engineers were already working feverishly on the next-generation Ford, the 1952 series, but first needed to bring the '51 model to market with even more changes—including Ford's first automatic transmission.

▶

Framed by the legendary Ford Rouge complex on the Rouge River in Dearborn, Michigan, this Deluxe Tudor reflected the new level of refinement incorporated into all 1951 Fords. (Photo: Henry Ford Museum and Ford Motor Company)

FORD

The Year 1951

This '51 convertible had a unique dealer modification replacing the spinner grille modules with amber fog lamps. The front bumper now had a small, flat indentation to accommodate states such as California that required front license plates.

Ford production was down 21 percent in 1951 due to material shortages and government limitations on production as the Korean War continued. Ford Division's market share dropped from 17.8 percent in 1950 to 16.9 percent in 1951. The Korean War had Ford gearing up once again to become a major equipment producer for the U.S. military. But unlike the situation in 1942, manufacturing and new model introductions continued at a feverish pace.

The 1951 models emphasized refinements throughout the lineup. Although body styles were still based on the 1949 models, the vehicles were superior in many ways. With many of the changes having taken place in 1950, the big news of '51 was the Fordomatic transmission.

The body changes included a dual-spinner grille, longer wraparound bumpers and a new location for the parking lamps. The models also had larger tail lamps. The rear deck lid was now counterbalanced and integrated a new key lock. Upholstery, headliner and interior trim color choices were greater than ever to harmonize with exterior colors.

The '51 models had a long production run of almost 17 months, with the first assemblies starting on October 4, 1950. The 1952 models didn't start production until March 10, 1952.

But despite the longer run, war restrictions kept the 1951 models from outselling their 1949 or 1950 model counterparts.

Products

The bread and butter of the Ford lineup for 1951 consisted of the Deluxe and Custom lines. Many of the manufacturers used the "ladder climbing" process of model names to bring new excitement into their lineups. For instance, in 1949 the Ford Deluxe was top of the line, in 1950 the Custom Deluxe was top dog and in 1951, the new Crestliner and Victoria models were the new range toppers. Each year that a new model was introduced, it effectively demoted the previous top model from that position. This enabled Ford to keep a model the public was familiar with, but still add a new and exciting model

every year if the company wanted that option.

The Crestliner, Country Squire and later the Victoria were stand alone models not falling under either the Deluxe or Custom banners. The Crestliner, introduced in July 1950, was a competitor of Chevrolet's new Bel Air, which was already showing great sales promise. Ford considered the Crestliner a holdover vehicle until they could introduce the sexy, new Victoria in January.

Deluxe, Custom and Station Wagon Models

The Deluxe lineup came in Tudor, Fordor and Business Coupe models. These were the low-priced entry vehicles that had the same running gear and underpinnings as more expensive models, but without extra trim and chrome. By reaching up one notch in the Custom line, a buyer could own a Club Coupe, Tudor, Fordor or a Convertible. Both the six-cylinder and the V-8 were available on all Tudor, Fordor, Club Coupe and Country Squire models, but the V-8 was the only choice for the Crestliner, Convertible and Victoria models.

One concern of the Ford marketing department was that the Chevy six produced almost the same power as the Ford V-8. The Ford engine produced more torque, provided better acceleration and had the V-8 "sound." The V-8 produced 100 horsepower and the six had 95. Because Chevy still only offered a six-cylinder engine, Ford had a sales and marketing advantage.

Convertible

Ford's Convertible was a great-looking flagship for the company. It was costly to design and build, and contributed only a small percentage to Ford's market share, but the image-maker brought people into showrooms, even if they left with a Fordor.

It only came with a V-8 engine (no mere six-cylinder was allowed under the hood), and the Convertible featured the motor-lift top with a switch located on the lower edge of the instrument panel, just to the left of the steering column. One flip of the switch and the ragtop lowered completely behind the rear seat. It was a hydraulic system with the pump located inside of the left-hand quarter panel.

Timeline

- American writer James Jones publishes the war novel, *From Here to Eternity*
- Auto racer Juan Manuel Fangio wins the world driving championship for the first time
- Boxer Sugar Ray Robinson defeats Jake La Motta for the middleweight title
- British Conservatives win a general election with Winston Churchill as leader
- Comedian Lucille Ball stars in the television series *I Love Lucy*
- Rodgers and Hammerstein's Broadway musical *The King and I* is produced
- Ten million television receivers have been installed in U.S. homes
- The first successful videotape for recording television images is demonstrated
- Color television goes on sale for the first time
- The Kaiser automobile features a padded dashboard and pop-out windshield
- Korean War metal restrictions announced by government

Ford saw marketing value in pitching the idea of more families owning two cars. The advertising suggested you could own two Fords for the price of one of the expensive brand vehicles. (Photo: Henry Ford Museum and Ford Motor Company)

The Country Squire station wagon had mahogany wood panels with either birch or maple framing. The wood was real, and therefore difficult to maintain or replace. With the high maintenance, real wood was now in its last year for Ford.

Many times amber fog lamps accessorized the front of a top-of-the-line new Ford. These were normally dealer-installed. Parking lights were kept in the same location but now a smaller, round shape instead of the horizontal format of 1950.

"From beauty to duty in just three minutes." The wagon could either haul eight passengers or with the seats folded down, would haul a thousand pounds of cargo.

Leather upholstery was relatively easy to keep because it could be wiped down with a damp cloth. However, it was also very hot to sit on during the summer months. The wide front seat provided easy seating for three.

Ford's all-new hood ornament appeared to be a combination of shark, jet and bird.

The split tail gate allowed easy loading and the window would latch into place once raised to stay out of the way.

The steering wheel was a fresh design for 1951 and the dash was similar to the sedans, but with a complete mahogany finish.

Country Squire Wagon

The Country Squire was the sole wagon offered in 1951 and was available only in a 2-door format. It was an 8-passenger wagon (three seats) with a one-half ton carrying capacity. Ford advertising described folding the rear seat down into the cargo mode as going "from beauty to duty in just three minutes." The rear seat had to be removed—no tools required—and the center seat folded down into the floor for a flat loading surface nine feet long. This was great for hauling kids, bikes, groceries or 2x4s—perfect for the middle-class American family. During long trips, the fold-down seats could also provide a sleeping area for the children.

Since 1949, the body was welded steel construction that was far more durable and squeak-free than the older woody models. It came with bolt-on mahogany side panels and either birch or maple framing. The tailgate was split into a lower half door that dropped down even with the loading area and the upper window section swung up out of the way. With the seats down, the wagon offered 38.8 square feet of loading space. The Country Squire was also available for the first time with an optional six-cylinder engine.

Crestliner

Crestliner was Ford's top-of-the-line sport coupe when it was introduced in July of 1950, and it came with limited two-tone body color combinations. Its purpose in life was to stem the tide of popularity for Chevy's sporty new Bel Air model, with its sports roof line, until the Victoria could make it to production some six months later. It was a rather strange-looking combination of paint schemes and trim, obviously pulled together quickly in an effort to fill a growing sales niche. The Crestliner was introduced as "the only one of its kind in the field," which was a true statement considering no other manufacturers cared to emulate it. Press releases described it as resembling European-style sports cars. Chances are no one from Europe would have described it that way.

The interior featured a two-tone dash with matching body color on top and the lower portion in satin black separated by a horizontal strip of chrome. A die-cast chrome "Crestliner" nameplate was mounted in the center of the dash. The steering wheel was a four-spoke with a script "F" on the horn button in the center. Bedford cord material was used on both the seats and the upper portion of the door panels.

Ford realized it needed a knockout sports model to compete with Chevy in sales and was working around the clock on the new Victoria model. Management knew the Crestliner was little more than a desperate effort to provide dealers with a sports coupe. And when the 1951 Vicky hit the market, it was an instant success.

The big selling F-1 pickup was still popular even though it was nearing the end of its run. The all-new models would show up in 1953.

Two power choices were still available for Ford customers—a 100 horsepower V-8 or a 95 horsepower inline six-cylinder.

Ford now had an integrated key lock and a counter balance for the rear deck lid.

Gear selector for the Fordomatic transmission was located just over the steering column.

The smooth, clean body design of the B-A series bodies was readily accepted by the public and Ford produced a total of 1,013,381 Ford cars in '51. A Ford Custom Tudor Sedan sold for $1584.

To harmonize with new exterior colors, interior trim color choices were greater than ever.

Back seat room was living room sized. Passenger pull-handles were mounted high to help entry and exit.

All models equipped with the Fordomatic had a chrome identfication badge under the Ford crest.

Victoria

The Ford Victoria was described by the *Detroit News* on January 28, 1951, as "the company's first model to combine the sports beauty of a convertible with the comforts of a closed sedan." Ford preferred to call it a "customized sedan," but whatever they called it, the Victoria was immensely popular and a badly needed competitor to go up against the Bel Air. What made this model an instant success was the new roofline that added a totally new and sporty look to a tiring Ford body design. It provided good looks and 7 ¼ square feet of glass space across the rear window.

The Victoria went into production during the first week of February 1951 and was priced $25 less than the standard Convertible. "The Victoria's styling and engineering make it a distinctive addition to our line of fine cars," said Ford Division General Manager L.D. Crusoe. The 6-passenger vehicle had armrests with ashtrays in the side and the rear quarter windows rolled completely down.

The sport coupe could be had with a manual transmission with optional overdrive or the new Fordomatic but came only with the 100-horsepower V-8 engine. No six was offered in this upscale model. The chassis was described as a double-drop frame with box section side rails. Lower flanges in the middle section of the frame were added for more strength.

The new model came with a choice of five single-tone colors or five two-tone combinations. The singles were Raven black, Alpine blue, Hawthorne green metallic, Sea Island green or Mexacalli maroon metallic. Two-tone combinations included a Hawaiian bronze metallic body and Sandpiper top, Alpine blue body with Silvertone gray top, Greenbrier metallic body with Sea Island green top, Island green

Belle of the Boulevard . . .

The stunning new

FORD *Victoria*

Greenbrier Metallic with Sea Island Green Top

New Victoria, with fresh pillarless hardtop styling, gave Ford a model to compete with Chevy's Bel Air.

body and Raven black top or Sportsman's green body and Raven black top.

The combination armrest and door grips were padded, covered with vinyl on the top and wool cloth on the lower portion, and separated with a chrome strip across the center. Front seats were stuffed with a foam rubber pad and nonsag springs.

Ford always liked to tag any new feature with a special name, such as "Centramatic" steering, "Double-Seal" hydraulic brakes, "Life Guard" body and "Power Cushion" clutch. The night lighting on the instrument panel was dubbed "Safety Glow."

"The Victoria carries out our policy of offering a selection of cars for every purpose with color and trim for every taste," said the division's sales manager L.W. Smead. The top-selling "convertible hardtop" models in 1950 were the Buick Riviera, Chevrolet Bel Air, Pontiac

1951 Model Car Pricing		
	Six-cylinder	V-8
Ford Deluxe		
Business Coupe	$1323	$1411
Tudor Sedan	$1416	$1491
Fordor Sedan	$1464	$1539
Ford Custom Deluxe		
Tudor Sedan	$1504	$1584
Fordor Sedan	$1504	$1539
Club Coupe	$1552	$1590
Convertible		$1948
Country Squire		
Wagon	$2029	$2109
Crestliner		$1595
Victoria*		$1925
The Victoria was introduced January 28, 1951, later than the other models		

Catalina, Oldsmobile Holiday and the Cadillac Coupe de Ville—all from General Motors. This totaled seven percent of GM's total car production that year, so Ford knew the importance of getting the '51 Victoria to dealers quickly. The Crestliner was continued until Victoria production was completely up to speed.

Styling Evolution

Six new body colors were offered for 1951 and a total of ten for all models except the Crestliner, with three colors, and the Convertible, with four two-tone combinations.

Ford also added a new winged hood ornament to accent the "look ahead" styling, even though this would be the last year for this body design. The grille was known as the "dual spinner" and Ford liked to call it "massive." It incorporated a new location for the parking lamps just below the horizontal center chrome bar.

The prices announced for the 1951 models on November 24, 1950, were widely covered in the press as being unchanged from the 1950 models. Ford Division head L.D. Crusoe announced that the company would not raise prices on the new model Ford cars. But by December 6, Ford jumped the prices by $92 across the board.

Gas mileage as tested by *Motor Trend* magazine in a 1951 article was 18.28 miles per gallon with a V-8 and automatic transmission. "The acceleration of the '51 Ford with Fordomatic doesn't exactly pin you to your seat, but it has more than average speed up and down the scale." They pitted their test vehicle against a manual 3-speed 1950 V-8 model and found them even in acceleration to 60 miles per hour.

The suspension was the same basic layout as the 1950 models but the front spring rate was softened and the rear shocks revalved to provide a more level ride. Performance of the V-8 was 17.8 seconds to 60 miles per hour and it achieved a top speed of 88 mph.

Popular Mechanics magazine printed a thorough Floyd Clymer

test of the 1951 Ford, which incorporated responses from more than 1,000 Ford owners in April, 1951. Most owners seemed to give high marks to the new Fordomatic transmission with comments such as, "The 1951 Ford is very stable at all speeds. Fordomatic seems to accelerate without too much slippage or engine speedup. It gets going quickly." One Kansas mail carrier said, "The Fordomatic has made my driving the easiest part of my job. The car is excellent."

The Fordomatic-equipped models averaged about 1.3 miles per gallon less than the manual transmission versions. Clymer reported, "If there ever has been any doubt about the loyalty of Ford owners, this survey should end it for all time. There were many kinks, as reported above, but in almost every case, between the lines was this sentiment: 'Even my best friend has a fault or two and I forgive him.'"

Aftermarket Add-Ons

There were many aftermarket suppliers during the 1950s to provide hundreds of accessories for new and used car buyers. Ford sanctioned some of the add-on items to be dealer-installed, Ford installed some items at the factory and the rest were available at local specialty shops or through mail order. One of the more popular add-on accessories was the continental kit (wheel carrier). This was considered quite stylish, and also gave the owner much additional luggage space in the trunk by relocating the spare tire.

Hudelson-Whitebone based in Champaign, Illinois, and San Francisco, California, was one of the companies producing continentals during the early '50s. Their ads billed it as being a distinctive "Look Ahead Feature" and adding a "richer, longer, wider appearance," becoming an integral part of the body. It added 25 percent more trunk space,

and Hudelson suggested that the now-empty tire well be used for tool storage. Their steel tire cover incorporated a license plate light, matching body paint and a permanent hubcap for a factory look. Opening the trunk required unlatching the spare wheel, letting it swing down to a horizontal position, and unlocking the trunk. Rubber grommets and weather seals were used to keep rattles, squeaks and vibration to a minimum.

Popular factory accessories included a Custom or Deluxe radio receiver, automatic pushbuttons for the radio, Magic Air heating and ventilating system, electric clock, cigarette lighter, courtesy and map light, spotlights and turn indicators.

Engineering Changes

Fordomatic Transmission

In 1948 Henry Ford II and Ernie Breech paid a visit to GM president C. E. Wilson about buying Hydra-matic transmissions from his company for their Lincolns. The GM head agreed to sell to them while Harold Youngren was back at Ford working hard to finish up the Fordomatic.

The new Ford-built 3-speed torque-converter automatic transmission for Ford and Mercury cars was announced by Youngren in October of 1949, however it wasn't installed in a vehicle until late 1950 for the 1951 model range.

The Borg-Warner Corporation did the development and production with Ford under a joint venture. The Mercury version was called the Merc-O-Matic. The extra cost option combined the advantages of a hydraulic torque converter and a planetary gear train to provide maximum performance and smooth shifting.

The popular dealer-installed continental kit added extra space for luggage. The tire housing would tilt back or to the side, depending on the manufacturer, to allow raising the trunk lid and loading cargo.

Rear seat room in the convertible was adequate because the wheel wells didn't intrude into the passengers' seating zone.

The 1949–50 hood ornaments were very similar. The 1951 version was very different with a forward looking jet-like design.

The convertible and station wagon frames were a heavier "X" pattern design for additional body stiffening. The sedans were a ladder-

The tail light lenses on the '51 models were wider than previous models and small, round backup lights were another dealer-installed

The gear selector, whether a manual transmission or Fordomatic, was located on the column. The dash layout was clean and simple, making

The F-6 Ford trucks were heavy haulers for the toughest of farm work. For any heavier work, you needed to move up to the Big Job F-8 model heavy duty trucks.

The basic principles for the Fordomatic transmission were formed in 1945. It would be a liquid-type torque converter. A number of types were tested, including both a wet and dry type friction-clutch transmission and also fluid-coupling combinations. But they all fell short, so Borg-Warner and Ford agreed to develop the torque converter with a 3-speed gear set operated hydraulically. An automatic shift from second gear to third happened anywhere from 15 to 60 miles per hour, depending on the amount of throttle pressure. Below 50 miles per hour, the transmission could downshift to second for passing or to use for compression breaking. The transmissions were all built both by Borg-Warner in Muncie, Indiana, and by Ford Motor

Company in Livernois, Michigan.

Overdrive was available as an option with the Fordomatic. It was operated by a t-handle just below the ventilation controls. By pulling out the handle, overdrive was turned off. Otherwise, the overdrive would kick in at speeds above 27 miles per hour.

One major glitch with the new Fordomatic transmission almost ruined its reputation during the first model year. The company had set up a long-term driving test with the Kansas City Police Department to compare maintenance costs of the Fordomatic versus manual transmissions. The manuals were notorious for clutch repair costs. During one service in which transmission fluid was drained, foreign metal shavings were discovered. After a full teardown

at the Ford transmission plant, it was found that the sleeve bearings in the transmissions all had failed. These had about 60,000 miles on them, but the company decided that this could happen as early as 10,000 miles.

The engineering staff quickly converted all production to needle, roller or ball bearings to solve the problem. In the meantime, Ford engineering decided it could expect the same to happen to possibly all customer Fordomatics with the sleeve bearings and should prepare for a replacement program. It was estimated that this could cost the company as much as $30 million, but would be necessary to protect the reputation of Ford and the new automatic transmission.

With Ernie Breech, Henry Ford II and L. D. Crusoe deeply

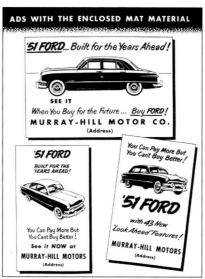

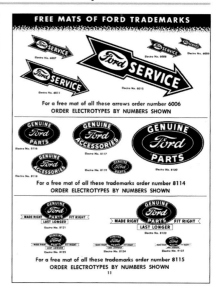

Advertising mats were a set of line-art drawings supplied by Ford Motor Company to the dealers, helping them to look and sound professional and to use consistent descriptions when describing the vehicles. The drawings, completely ready for newspapers to use, made it easy for dealers to look good and mat packages generally included radio spots in 10, 15 and 30 second formats as well. All the dealer had to do was give the radio script to the station, have their readers put it on the air and they were in business.

concerned, it was finally decided that rebuilt transmissions with the new bearings would be provided to customers who had a problem with their Fordomatics. This would be prorated according to mileage at minimal cost to the customer. As it turned out, the transmissions were apparently tougher than anyone guessed, and with fewer returns than expected, the company costs didn't approach the original projections. Customers with transmission problems were well taken care of.

One Ford zone sales manager from Milwaukee pointed out that some dealer salespersons took great delight in shifting the new automatic from forward to reverse—while in forward motion! Fortunately, much of this was done in the winter on snow and ice, causing little damage, but engineering soon added an "inhibitor" to prevent drivers from this style of shifting.

Minor Detail Changes

Rear deck lids were now being counterbalanced and spring-loaded to pop up when the key was turned. The lid would easily stay in position when raised.

The Safety Glow instrument panel included a unique speedometer pointer with a glowing ring circling and illuminating the number indicating the speed. One magazine report gave a "thumbs down" to the circular needle, saying it obscured the reading on the speedometer.

The instrument panel knobs for the radio and various other controls were now recessed into the dash to inhibit the chance that occupants might be impaled on them in a crash. These knobs were made of white plastic and back-lit to reveal the name of each control in low light. These were some of the earlier Ford efforts at promoting safety in their automobiles.

Key-starting with the new ignition switch was a fresh idea for 1951. Previous models required turning the key and pressing the start button in two separate actions. The new method provided the driver with a one-operation start process. The adjustable sliding front seat was mounted on curved tracks to provide the "correct position for tall or short drivers." The seat was spring-assisted to pull the seat forward during adjustment.

Performance Assurance Hints

Have your car checked and greased periodically with the 1,000-mile "Performance Assurance" operation.

Every spring and fall, have a complete check-up and lubrication change; including a change of engine oil, by ordering the 5,000-mile "Performance Assurance" job from your Dealer.

Once a year, the 10,000-mile "Performance Assurance" operation should be performed to restore your car to that "like-new" condition.

Take advantage of the free service offered by gas stations whenever you stop for fuel. Have the attendant check the oil level, tire pressures, the battery for low water and the radiator coolant level.

Advertising and Promotion

Ford sent free advertising mats to dealers. These were sheets of quality paper stock with line drawings and text ready to send to newspapers for their advertising. These also included suggested scripts for radio spots, ranging from 10 seconds to 30 seconds.

10 and 15 seconds:
- "See the new '51 Ford today. It's built for the years ahead! Now on display at (Dealer's name)."
- "Join the crowds going to (Dealer's name) to see the '51 Ford . . . the car that's built for the years ahead!"

30 seconds:
- "If you're one of the smart buyers who are looking to the years ahead—buying for the future—you'll surely want to see the new '51 Ford at (Dealer's name). This is the car that's built for the years ahead, with 43 "Look Ahead" features and the sensational new Fordomatic Drive. Visit (Dealer's name) today and see this great new Ford. When you see it, you'll agree, "You can pay more . . . but you can't buy better!"

Wrapping up the 1951 model year, Ford learned that due to the national emergency of the Korean War, total vehicle production dropped 21 percent as it geared up to start once again producing products to support the government. But the 1951 Fords were one of the best values on the market because most of the problems, bugs and glitches were corrected and the quality levels were much higher than before.

Now that Ford was ready to introduce its next all-new design, the only worry was doing it in the midst of the war efforts and government-enforced production cutbacks.

Warranties

In the early 1950s, warranties didn't match up to what we are used to today. The only competition was from the other two big American producers, who had similar warranties. A new Ford vehicle was under a very basic limited warranty, for only 90 days from purchase or 4,000 miles—whichever came first. And this covered only the actual replacement part. The owner still had to pay for shipping. Outlined below is the text from page 33 of the 1951 Ford Owner's Manual:

"The Ford Motor Company warrants all such parts of new automobiles, trucks and chassis, *except* tires, for a period of ninety (90) days from the date of original delivery to the purchaser of each new vehicle or before such vehicle has been driven 4,000 miles, whichever event shall first occur, as shall, under normal use and service, appear to it to have been defective in workmanship or material. This warranty shall be limited to shipment, to the purchaser without charge, except for transportation, of the part or parts intended to replace those acknowledged by the Ford Motor Company to be defective. The Ford Motor Company cannot, however, and does not accept any responsibility in connection with any of its automobiles, trucks or chassis when they have been altered outside of its own factories or branch plants. If the purchaser shall use or allow to be used in the automobile, truck or chassis, parts not made or supplied by the Ford Motor Company, then this warranty shall become void. This warranty is expressly in lieu of all other warranties expressed or implied and all other obligations or liabilities on the part of Ford Motor Company, and no person including any dealer, agent, or representative of the Ford Motor Company is authorized to make any representation or warranty concerning Ford Motor Company products on behalf of the Company except to refer purchasers to this warranty.

The Ford Motor Company reserves the right to make changes in design and changes or improvements upon its products without imposing any obligation upon itself to install the same upon its products theretofore manufactured."

The owner's manual also promoted Ford's Performance Assurance "hints." They wanted to keep the customer happy with a good running car, and the dealer happy with scheduled maintenance to keep its staff busy. This included regular oil changes at 5,000-mile intervals and of course, those "free services" offered by all gas stations.

The 1951 F-1 pickups had the same flathead six-cylinder or V-8 options as the cars.

▶

The Mainline was the entry series for 1952. This Tudor model sold for $1555 with a V-8 and 79,931 were produced that year. (Photo: Henry Ford Museum and Ford Motor Company)

FORD

The Year 1952

All-New Cars, Government Restrictions and Bigger Market Share

The company's financial results in 1952 were considerably less profitable than previous years, thanks to the worsening of the Korean War and limits by the NPA (National Production Authority) on supply of materials and the number of vehicles Ford could produce. Profits were also affected by a two-month steel strike that began June 2, and downtime due to a major model changeover as the new 1952 Fords came on-line.

Production in 1952 was down 16 percent, at 1,323,578 units (1,580,704 in 1951 and a post-war record of 2,000,495 in 1950) although net income was only down about $10 million for the year. Ford Division had healthy car sales, limited only by government restrictions, moving up from a 16.9 to a 17.9 percent market share, while Chevrolet dropped from 21.1 to 20.5 percent, placing Ford soundly in second position in the industry with an eye on Chevy. Ford was also spending $1.1 billion in 1952 for property, new facilities and equipment.

Ford trucks were basically a carryover for 1952. The company always introduced new truck and car models in different years.

The Crestline Victoria along with the Sunliner topped the sex appeal list of the Ford lineup in 1952. With an all-new line of body styles, Ford had managed to stay ahead of its chief rival, Chevrolet, in the style game.

This helped give each vehicle its own publicity, letting it shine without having to fight the other for editorial space. It also helped not to burden the company's engineering, design and marketing staffs, letting them focus on one or the other, but not all at once in the same year.

Everyone was scrambling to get a dealership to sell the new Ford products, but with the economy slowing and the Korean War gaining momentum, the number of dealers would decline by almost 50 by the next year.

Ford Sales

Ford was selling all of its new '52 models it could produce. Between the government restrictions and the steel strike, the company couldn't keep up with demand. The dealers were as well organized and profitable as they had ever been, but just couldn't get enough of the new vehicles. Although frustrating to Ford, they at least had comfort in knowing that all the other manufacturers were

more or less in the same boat. Ford's all-new models were hot items on the market, and Ford was hoping to make serious inroads against Chevrolet this year. But instead of complaining, Henry stepped up to the plate and sent a letter to the president, saying that Ford was ready to do its part in production to support the war effort. "What is required?" was his only question.

New design

Another All-New, Walker-Designed Ford

The completely new George Walker-designed 1952 Ford was introduced to the public in the spring of 1951. It was again a hit and the new body design promised a much tighter fit to rid Ford of the squeaks-and-rattles reputation that plagued earlier models. Part of the tighter fit came from a stiffer body. It had rounded corners wherever possible, extra welds and generally better engineering. The 1949 to 1951 models suffered from a number of inherent problems, including poor body fits that enabled dust and moisture to enter the interior. With the new model, the company seemed to move beyond those problems.

A new six-cylinder engine, an all-steel-bodied 2- or 4-door wagon, suspended brake and clutch pedals, center-mounted gas filler and a one-piece curved front windshield were other highlights in the new lineup.

The six-cylinder overhead-valve engine had been under development for several years, along with a new V-8, but when the United States became involved in the Korean War and manufacturers started halting projects, the V-8 was delayed. Fortunately, the six-cylinder was ready and made it into production.

Performance became a problem for Ford. The new Mileage Maker Six engine was outperforming the flathead V-8! Well-known *Mechanix Illustrated*

writer Tom McCahill loved Fords and had a no-nonsense style when describing what he did or didn't like. Testing the new overhead-valve six version of the '52 Ford, he said, "This current job is pure, unadulterated dynamite with a conventional transmission or overdrive."

He enjoyed the 3-speed manual transmission, but had harsh words for the six with a Fordomatic. "The Ford six with Fordomatic reminded me of running an outboard through a lake of molasses in January. Zero to 60 with the contraption took 16.1 seconds, or nearly four seconds longer than with the regular shift."

McCahill said there was only one thing that would make Ford owners wince. The new Ford six engine resembled an overgrown Chevrolet six. He tested top speed at the Dearborn Proving Grounds test track at 94 miles per hour. The manual 3-speed accelerated from zero to 60 mph in 12.3 seconds.

Timeline

- Chuck Yeager sets a new air speed record of 1,650 mph in the X-1A research plane
- Dancer Gene Kelly stars in the film *Singin' in the Rain*
- Eva Peron, popularly known as Evita, dies in Argentina of ovarian cancer
- Gary Cooper and Grace Kelly star in the Western film *High Noon*
- The United States tests the first hydrogen bomb in the Pacific
- Major steel strike stops production at most auto plants
- The first automatic pin-setter is installed in a bowling alley in Brooklyn, New York
- Richard Nixon gives his famous "Checkers" speech on TV
- NBC's *Today* show pioneers the morning news-show format
- Movie of the year: *The Greatest Show on Earth*

Products

Three Model Lines

1952's all-new body designs were offered in three basic lines: Mainline, Customline and Crestline.

Classified as a light truck, the Courier was marketed as a small business vehicle for florists, grocery delivery and other light-duty needs. Only 6,225 Couriers were produced in 1952. (Photo: Henry Ford Museum and Ford Motor Company)

The new Ford body design still had a carry-over theme with the center chrome spinner and parking lights. Although the Lincoln saw new improvements such as a slick new independent front suspension and an overhead-valve V-8, due to the cutbacks in materials and production during the Korean War, the Fords wouldn't see this for two model years.

The Crestline and V-8 emblems were always mounted to the front fender, letting anyone know that this was the top-of-the-line model. The V-8 or six-cylinder engines ran equally well, but the six was available only in the lower-priced Mainline and Customline series. Crestline models all came with a V-8 only.

The chrome bumper guard on this Victoria was typical of a dealer installed accessory. The spinner theme was continued with the new models with the center grille and parking lamps.

The Coronado deck conversion was a popular option for the '52 model Fords. It was a looks-only option available from dealers. The full-size spare was located in the trunk and key access was through the chrome center of the Coronado wheel cover. The extended license plate swung down to

All gauges and column shifter (for manual or Fordomatic) were within easy reach of the driver. The clock was centered on the dash for viewing

Although the new overhead-valve six-cylinder produced almost as much horsepower as the "Strato-Star" flat-head, the sales still went heavily to

In the entry-level Mainline model, customers had the choice of a three-seat Business Coupe, Tudor sedan, Fordor sedan and a 2-door Ranch Wagon with all-steel construction. Customline offered Tudor and Fordor sedans, a Club Coupe and a 4-door Country Sedan Wagon. The top-of-the-line Crestline came in a Victoria hardtop, a Sunliner convertible and a Country Squire Wagon with wood side trim.

All wagons had a "stowaway" center seat and the Crestline model came equipped with a two-piece removable rear seat. All had a counterbalanced liftgate for easy loading and access.

Although the '52 models had a sexy new body they had gained some weight and were now up to 3,210 pounds for the six-cylinder model and at 3,390 for the V-8. The '49 six-cylinder models weighed in at 3,150 pounds, so a combination of efforts to increase quality by using heavier parts and improve the ride and noise characteristics on the new model contributed to a heavier, poorer-handling vehicle. With less overall weight and less weight on the front wheels, the six-cylinder OHV model was often chosen as the best of the two models in magazine road tests when rated for handling and acceleration.

In a *Road & Track* magazine (April, 1952) road test, writer Oliver Billingsley reported, "For the average American family, Ford has produced a car which will please their taste and satisfy their demands. The six with standard transmission is my choice . . ." One of his co-testers, Bill Brehaut, felt the designers had gone "all-out for a comfortable ride and that big-car feel." He said, "To the old-time Ford fans who liked Fords because of their light weight and sparkling performance, even at a sacrifice in finish and comfort, this car will be a great disappointment." Maybe the vehicle was

Handsome and handy is the new Ford Country Sedan! Use it to tote 8 people in style or a half ton of freight! The back seat lifts right out, the center seat folds flush with the floor! Powered by 110-h.p. Strato-Star V-8, Fordomatic or Overdrive if you choose.

We call this 4-door beauty the Country Squire. You'll call it wonderful. Has all the new Country Sedan features . . . plus real maple or birch trim, framing mahogany-finished steel panels.

What a car – what a value! It's the 2-door Ranch Wagon . . . the lowest priced station wagon in its field . . . with a choice of 110-h.p. Strato-Star V-8 or 101-h.p. Mileage Maker Six.

Whichever Ford station wagon you choose you're hitched to a star with more "can do" than any other in the low-price field!

the greatest line of station wagons in the industry

WOWING 'EM EVERYWHERE! '52 FORD

You can pay more but you can't buy better!

heavier and not quite as nimble, but the overall quality, tightness and ride were far superior to what Ford owners had experienced before.

The ride of the new Ford was comparable to some of the best American automobiles built during 1952, which was certainly one of Ford's engineering goals. A wraparound windshield and larger side and rear windows greatly improved visibility. Soft green tinted safety glass was optional. Dual windshield wipers were standard along with a locking glove box in the dash, new contour-style seats and a wraparound dash with colors to blend with the interior fabrics.

1952 Model Car Pricing		
	Six-cylinder	V-8
Mainline		
Business Coupe	$1389	$1459
Tudor Sedan	$1485	$1555
Fordor Sedan	$1530	$1600
Ranch Wagon	$1832	$1902
Customline		
Tudor Sedan	$1570	$1640
Fordor Sedan	$1615	$1649
Club Coupe	$1579	$1685
Country Sedan Wagon		$2060
Crestline		
Victoria		$1925
Sunliner Convertible		$2027
Country Squire Wagon		$2186

BIG '52 FORD

GREATEST
CAR EVER
BUILT
IN THE
LOW-PRICE
FIELD

This brochure featured the "Big '52 Ford," which truly was big, weighing in at almost 200 pounds more than the 1949 model cars. The Customline Tudor shown here could be purchased with a V-8 for $1640. Keep in mind that all suggested retail prices up until the 1959 models were shown only to the dealers. This all changed with the Monroney bill, which provided window stickers for the first time in 1959.

Accessories

Dealers continued to offer a number of accessory add-ons. These included the Auto-Wipe windshield washer (foot-pedal-sprayed washer fluid and wipers came on automatically), turn signals ("You won't have to open the window anymore!"), spotlights, outside rear-view mirrors, seven-tube custom radios, fender skirts, the always-popular wheel carrier—better known as a continental kit, and the ever-present Magic Air system.

A new accessory for '52 was the Coronado Deck. This was an alternative to the continental kit, which was still available. The Coronado Deck gave a "built-in" effect but actually had no tire in it, obviating the need for an extended bumper. The appearance-only accessory left the spare tire in the original trunk location and provided access through a hinged door in the center of the stainless-steel cap to the deck-lid lock. It also had a special license plate frame that would pull out for access to the new center-fill fuel cap. The purpose of the new-style deck kit was to get away from the cumbersome continental kit, which added ample extra weight off the end of the rear bumper and adversely affected handling characteristics. The Coronado, being a looks-only item, improved the cosmetics and kept weight down. It was also easy to install, with minimal modification to the body.

Aftermarket companies making continental kits still flourished, offering the alternative of more trunk space. Hollywood-based Auto Metal Products' ad in *Automotive News* said, "There's a tire mount in every Ford's future, and it means present profits for you!" This was a pitch for dealers to sell and install their kits locally. The kits cost the dealer $135 plus shipping, included a tire casing that could be painted to match the car, even in two-tones. No deck lid modifications were required and the tire carrier mounted directly to the frame. All bumper extension pieces were included.

Engineering Changes

Tighter Body Design

The bodies on the 1949 to 1951 models had been plagued with ill-fitting pieces that let dust and moisture enter the interior on a regular basis. One of the prime goals in redesigning the 1952 models was to overcome this problem and improve Ford's reputation.

To help separate the old bodies and their problems from the new lineup for 1952, marketing came up with a name to identify the new bodies. If it said "Coachcraft," you knew it was a new design and had a tight fit.

The bodies now had a curved, one-piece windshield. Door openings, footings and upper pillar joints were rounded to increase strength and promote positive sealing. Doors were hinged in a way that allowed adjustment for a tighter fit.

Even the floor pans were welded to the sills and rear wheelhouses to seal against dust and water leaks. A one-piece dash was welded to the cowl panels, both to cut squeaks and rattles and to give a better weather seal.

The frame-to-body bolts were insulated to keep down road noise and reduce vibration and harshness transmitted into the cabin.

Engines

The big story for 1952, second only to the new body design, was the overhead-valve six-cylinder—the first of this design in the Ford lineup. The new Mileage Maker inline six made its debut with 101 horsepower model and a 7.0:1 compression ratio.

The four-main-bearing six-cylinder now performed about as well as the trusty old flathead Strato-Star V-8 and got better mileage to boot. So Ford gave the

Mid-level Customline Fords were identifiable by the chrome strip on the fender. The Crestlines also had the chrome trim, but had only three models: Sunliner, Country Squire and Victoria. (Photo: Henry Ford Museum and Ford Motor Company)

V-8 a 10-percent horsepower boost (to 110) to give customers a reason to continue buying it.

The V-8 horsepower gain came primarily from an increase of compression from 6.8:1 to 7.2:1, a redesigned camshaft and a new Holley carburetor.

Six or V-8?

In a May, 1952, *Motor Trend* article by Walt Woron, a new Ford six and a V-8 were pitted against each other to see which was the better value. The test results found that the six-cylinder accelerated

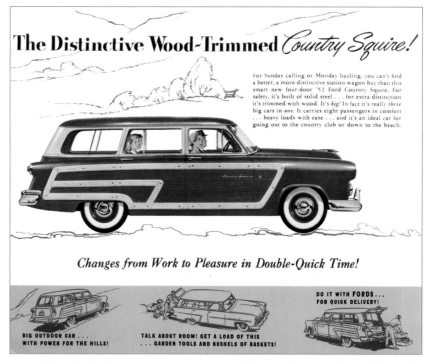

Although the Ford wagons have been widely described as "all steel" for 1952, they had actually been structurally all-steel since 1949. The Country Squire model did change to a decal in place of the previous Mahogany wood panels, but Ford kept the real Birch trim in place, so it wasn't a totally steel wagon just yet.

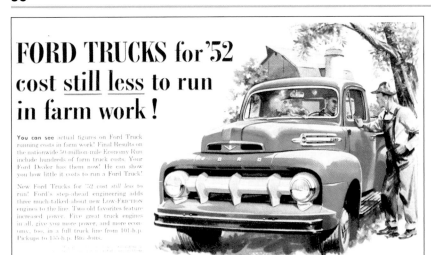

almost a full second faster to 60 mph than the V-8 and the mileage was almost identical. The new overhead-valve design in the six gave obvious advantages and Ford was trying to make the V-8 last until the introduction of the new OHV version due out in late 1953 (1954 models) by adding the extra ten horses.

The _Motor Trend_ writer described it like this: "The Eight has been developed; the Six is to be developed. One is the engine of the future; the other is that of the past. As they stand today, performance is equal, and you have to decide on one of these alternatives, if you're going to buy a Ford. I can stick with the V-8 which has been tried and proved reliable by tens of millions of owners, but which still isn't a top-efficiency engine, or I'll take my stand with the more modern, easier-to-work-on, more-efficient unit."

Motor Trend liked much of what it saw of the new Fords overall, but heavily criticized the steering for being sloppy. "This sloppiness in the steering is reflected in overall road behavior. While the springing of the car is really quite good and there is practically no body roll during high-speed cornering, the steering comes along and upsets the car's stability in a way that can be very disturbing and actually unsafe." But in the same article, the magazine raved about the brakes

on the new Ford, saying, "Ford's brakes are among the best we've ever tested. Remarkably enough, there was no tendency of the brakes to fade even during the severest punishment. Too, with all four wheels locked up tight at 60 mph, the six came to a fast stop in a perfectly straight line!"

The clutch and brake pedals were for the first time suspended from above to eliminate the floor holes that were a source of moisture, dust and noise— especially as the rubber seals on the previous models started to wear.

The six-cylinder, according to _Motor Trend_, turned in a zero to 60 mph acceleration run at 19.4 seconds, while the V-8 stood at 20.4 seconds. This was substantially slower than the acceleration figures turned in by McCahill at _Mechanix Illustrated_. Top speed was 93 mph for both. All new models now had a 115-inch wheelbase, one inch longer than earlier models, and a wider front track at 58 inches and a rear track of 56 inches, adding to overall stability.

1952 Ford Trucks

The F-1 pickup production for 1952 was more than 108,000 units, more than one third of Ford's total truck production. The trucks didn't change much from the earlier models except for offering a different grille and exterior trim.

Cleveland Engine Plant Opens

The ground breaking for the Cleveland Engine Plant had taken place in 1950. A foundry was also started on-site to support production of the new six-cylinder overhead-valve engine. The plant was complete by January, 1952, and while production started on the new six-cylinder, another line was being put in place for the

Ford pickups also got the new overhead-valve six-cylinder as the standard powerplant for 1952 with the V-8 as an option. Sales declined as the press was reporting that an all-new 1953 model would be revealed in the fall.

all-new overhead-valve V-8 engine that would start production in late 1953. Castings were purchased from an outside supplier until mid-year, when the Cleveland Foundry started producing castings for the engine plant.

Some forms of automated manufacturing had been around for many years, but now it was being applied to full-line mass production at Ford. For instance, at the Cleveland Engine Plant, 41 inline transfer machines were lined up in a continuous process 1,200 feet long with a worker touching the block only once, to load it onto the line. Under the old, manual process, 150 machines would have been in place with a person physically moving the

F-1 pickups would easily seat three across, and many farmers regularly hauled the whole family with four-across and the rest in the bed! The dash layout was basically unchanged from the 1951 models and the clutch, brake and gas pedals—like the '51 cars—were still floor mounted.

You're in good hands at your Ford Dealer's

There's something special about the service attention you receive from your Ford Dealer.

It's more than just the work of a Ford-trained mechanic. It's more than the stock of Genuine Ford Parts a Ford Dealer has on hand... and it's more than

just his knowledge of Ford-approved methods and Ford-right tools. It's the satisfied feeling you gain from dealing with folks you know, folks whose future is wrapped up in your Ford.

You and your Ford are truly in good hands at your Ford Dealer's.

Sure signs of savings

FORD DIVISION OF FORD MOTOR COMPANY
Fifty Years Forward on the American Road

Service had been identified as a key concern of many new car buyers. They wanted to know what they could expect from their dealers after the purchase, so Ford launched an advertising campaign to instill confidence by showing families, especially children, interfacing with service managers at Ford dealers.

block to each station during production. This saved Ford many man-hours and increased engine production greatly. Other departments in the Cleveland and Dearborn engine plants were also being automated during this period as Ford moved to become more efficient and profitable.

In Wayne, Michigan, the Wayne Assembly Plant opened to produce both Lincoln and Mercury lines as well as aircraft parts for the war effort.

Military Support

Ford Defense Contracts at $1.7 Billion

Ford continued to support government efforts in the Korean War, increasing military production in providing aircraft and tank engines, rockets and various other defense supplies. By March, the company was starting delivery of the R-4360 Pratt and Whitney aircraft engines being built in a Chicago government-

leased plant. The building was described as the world's largest factory under one roof. By July, the first B-36 bombers with all Ford engines began flying from Carswell Air Force Base in Fort Worth. This plant later converted production to Pratt and Whitney's new J-57 jet aircraft engine. Parts for the J-40 Westinghouse jet engines were being produced at the Wayne Assembly Plant (Wayne, Michigan) and then shipped to Chicago.

In Kansas City, Missouri, Ford started production of B-47 bomber wings. Spanning 68 feet long and weighing 7,000 pounds each, the wing assemblies were shipped to Boeing, Douglas and Lockheed assembly sites. In the Rouge Plant, 950 employees were working to assemble 500-horsepower V-8 tank engines. At about the same time, the Ford Engine and Foundry Division developed and produced a high-speed machine gun for the Army Ordnance engineers.

Going into late 1952, as Ford readied for production of the 1953 models, the company reported lower profits. Factors in this profit decline included lower production due to the war, the change over to the new '52 cars earlier in the year and to the all-new 1953 model trucks coming late in 1952. But the company had also picked up almost two full percentage points of market share over 1951, showing that it was making the right decisions.

▶

The Ford Rotunda building was moved from Chicago to Dearborn after the World's Fair in 1936. The Rotunda featured holiday scenes, a Teflon "ice rink" and a car testing road featuring surfaces from 17 famous roads around the world. It burned in 1962, never to be rebuilt. (Photo: Henry Ford Museum and Ford Motor Company)

FORD

The Year 1953

Ford Celebrates 50 Years

All government production limitations were lifted on February 13, 1953, with the end of the Korean War. This gave Ford Motor Company the chance to prove what it could do with its reorganized company and modernized facilities.

Ford dealerships had grown from 5,800 in 1941 to 6,609 in 1953. Total Ford Motor Company dealerships, including all Lincoln-Mercury outlets, stood at an all-time high of 8,339.

Another event of immediate importance to Ford in 1953 was its 50th anniversary on June 16. Ford's director of public relations, Charles Moore, was planning a number of events from early 1952. Moore had worked with Henry Ford's public relations man, Earl Newsom, before joining Ford. Anniversary events included:

- **The Ford Rotunda.**
  The Rotunda reopened after being closed during the Korean War.
- **Norman Rockwell paintings.**
  The company incorporated a series of Norman Rockwell paintings into its advertising campaigns.
- *Ford at Fifty.*
  Ford commissioned publication of a hardbound book about the company.

The Customline vehicles could be easily spotted by the long chrome strip running down the side of the front fenders. Tudor, Fordor and Club Coupe versions could be had with either a six-cylinder or V-8.

- **TV salute.** Ed Sullivan gave a special anniversary salute to Ford on the June 14 *Toast of the Town* show.
- **Special automobile feature.** "50th-anniversary" horn buttons for all 1953 model vehicles. Production started December 10, 1952.
- **Network special.** NBC and CBS television networks both carried an hour-long special on June 15, *America of the Past Fifty Years,* featuring Ford Motor Company in front of approximately 60 million viewers. Stars included Edward R. Murrow, Ethel Merman, Lowell Thomas and Mary Martin.

On May 20, 1953, President Eisenhower dedicated the new Research and Engineering Center (across from the Henry Ford Museum in Dearborn) in memory of Henry and Edsel Ford and to celebrate the company's 50th anniversary. Eisenhower wasn't actually present, but delivered his speech to Ford management through closed-circuit television from his White House office. This large, campus-like grouping of buildings included the famous 295,000 square-foot Ford Styling Building with its twelve studios reserved for building full-size clay models.

Construction of three major new plants in Louisville, Kentucky; San Jose, California; and Mahwah, New Jersey, also started in 1953. Ernie Breech broke ground for the Central Staff Office Building, later named Ford World Headquarters. It was anticipated that the headquarters building would be completed by 1955, but completion was delayed until September, 1956. (In 1998, this building was renamed the Henry Ford II World Center.)

Sales for 1953 were good, with 1903 to 1953 total production reaching an incredible 45 million units. Ford described this as enough vehicles end-to-end to reach around the Earth more than four times. Total production for 1953 alone was 1,247,542.

Ford at Fifty

Henry Ford II commissioned the book, *Ford at Fifty,* to celebrate the 50th anniversary of Ford Motor Company. He asked a former managing editor of *Life* magazine to assemble the best writers, photographers and editors to put the publication together, and Simon & Schuster of New York agreed to publish it.

A loose letter from Henry II was tucked inside the first page of each copy of the book. The letter explained why the book had been written and what Ford hoped to accomplish with it.

"One of the first things we decided to do when we began to plan our 50th Anniversary was to publish a book about Ford Motor Company today told in terms of people. Of course, it would be impossible to tell the story about every phase of the company's activities in one book, but we knew we could show a lot about the kind of people who work with us and the things they do.

About a year ago, we asked the former managing editor of Life *magazine to come in and put the book together for us. He and his staff, composed of some of the best photographers, writers and artists in the country, produced the story and pictures you will find in* Ford at Fifty. *When they finished the job, we felt it was not only a fine portrait of our company, but of a segment of American life as well.*

"I am happy to send you this copy of Ford at Fifty *and I hope you and your family will enjoy reading it."*

The first 17 pages of the book were dedicated to Sacramento, California, a city that was perceived to epitomize the booming American city on wheels. Sacramento had grown from a population of 170,000 to 316,000 in only 12 years, and the story focused on how the automobile had helped to change the quality of life for the inhabitants. The people of Sacramento drove a million miles per day in 1953. Many drive-up-window businesses, including dry cleaners, hamburger stands, fortune tellers, book drop-offs, mail boxes and utility pay windows were available for drivers so they would have no need to leave their cars.

The book told the story of Henry Ford, the Rouge manufacturing site, the making of steel and how Ford cars were then made. Individual employees and people were photographed and called out by name in the book, bringing a personal touch to Ford and all its employees. The last sections included cars for the future, the new Ford Motor Company, defense work, the company and the community.

The inside front cover featured a beautiful series of ribbons across the pages with illustrations of vehicles ranging from the 1903 Model A to the then-new 1953 F-100 pickup. There was even a hint of a line drawing indicating a vehicle that might be on the horizon, just after the new-pickup illustration. The book was sent to owners and dealers throughout the United States.

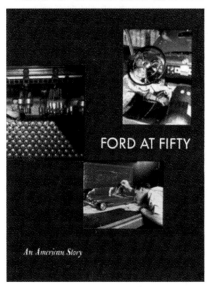

The premiere Ford Motor Company publication, put together by a former managing editor of Life *magazine, was available for $2.95, and was also sent free to fleet buyers and premium customers. This publication is now rare. It depicted American life in 1953 as it related to Ford and the automotive industry.*

The top-of-the-line Country Squire wagon sold for $2556, almost $200 more than the Sunliner convertible. The "wood grain" body panels were now imitation wood, while the trim still came in Birch. (Photo: Henry Ford Museum and Ford Motor Company)

The "Flight Control" wrap-around dash in this Sunliner kept all controls close to the driver, including the control for the hydraulic powered automatic top. All '53 models had an anniversary horn button. The horn ring for '53 went back to a half circle from the full circle in '52. The dash layout remained basically unchanged. By 1953 most manufacturers had the key on the right side of the steering column, but Ford still stuck to its traditional left-side key start.

Leather seats in the Sunliner were comfortable and stylish.

The rear seats in the Sunliner were wide enough to comfortably seat three people as the wheel wells didn't intrude.

The Ford crest was now a part of the Ford family of cars since its 1950 introduction. With the close of the Korean War, Ford sold over 1.2 million cars in 1953—double the 671,733 sold the previous year. Sunliner production went from 22,000 units in '52 to 40,000 units in 1953.

Fender skirts were an option on the Sunliners. The 1953 trim included stainless-steel pieces on the rear fender bulge on all Crestliners.

The exterior of the '53 had only trim changes including the new shape and placement of the parking lights in place of the "spinners." The Sunliner went for $2042 and came with a leather trimmed interior.

The Rouge red flathead V-8 engine was still by far the most popular engine in the Ford line and standard on any Crestline series car.

The Ford Rotunda

The Ford Rotunda was built as the Ford exhibit for the 1934 World's Fair in Chicago, where more than 12 million people viewed Ford products and learned about the company. In 1935, Ford moved the gear-shaped structure to Dearborn where it was rebuilt as a welcoming center for people coming to visit the Rouge Plant and as a display for information about Ford products and facilities.

It was placed on a site across from the Administration Building (the original headquarters for Ford Motor Company) near the Rouge Plant. Known as "The gateway to the Rouge," the Rotunda was Detroit's biggest tourist attraction before closing during World War II. In 1950, the 15-year-old building underwent a complete restoration with the Buckminster Fuller Company designing a weather-break dome to span the Rotunda's 93-foot inner court. The new dome was made of nylon and plastic, supported by aluminum struts

and weighed 26,000 pounds. It would support almost ten times its own weight, typically as a snow or ice load during one of Dearborn's winters. Two outer wings of the building housed an auditorium and public relations offices.

It reopened to the public on June 16, 1953, to celebrate Ford's anniversary. An article in the June 19, 1953, *Ford Rouge News* said, "Golden floodlights and 50 huge candles made the circular exhibition building resemble a giant birthday cake. A special device used atomic radiation to light the building and the candles." Atomic radiation might not be the best description to use today, but it must have seemed futuristic at the time.

Displays at the Rotunda included manufacturing of raw materials into products, vehicle development—from drawings to final product—as well as scientific research helping to enrich American life. These exhibits gave visitors simple explanations of how the company strove to design and build better products.

There were 12 gigantic photos reaching completely around the Rotunda interior walls, each measuring from 20 to 42 feet wide and depicting life at Ford Motor Company. Sixteen large sculptured reliefs by Birmingham, Michigan, sculptor Marshall Fredericks also were on display in the building, portraying some of the basic industries that provided materials to the automotive industry.

The Rotunda's Michigan site was a 13 1/2-acre parcel of Ford property. It featured a test-drive road with 17 different surfaces representing famous roads of the world from various times in history. This was designed to show how highway construction has advanced and how modern Ford products provide a superior ride on almost any surface.

The famous road surfaces included:

Road	Country
1. Appian Way	Italy
2. Chausse D'Aerschot	Belgium
3. Diamond Rush Road	South Africa
4. Western Highway	Australia
5. Oregon Trail	United States
6. The Tokaida	Japan
7. Vaughn Plank Road	Canada
8. Lincoln Highway	United States
9. Boston Post Road	United States
10. Dixie Highway	United States
11. Grand Trunk Road	India
12. Watling Street	England
13. Cortez Road	Mexico
14. Woodward Avenue	United States
15. Summer Palace Road	China
16. Bergstrasse	Germany
17. Route De Quarante Sous	France

Postscript

The Rotunda building was undergoing roof repairs in November, 1962, when it caught fire and burned to the ground.

Approximately 60 percent of Ford's annual Christmas decorations were already in place and lost. No one was injured, but the building was a total loss and never rebuilt. In 1999, Ford opened to the public an all-new Spirit of Ford Building, a 21st-century version of the Rotunda, on a site across from the Henry Ford Museum.

Products

The car lineup for 1953 was a freshened version of the all-new line introduced the previous year. With eight body styles and three basic model lines, Ford offered more choices than archrival Chevrolet, and Ford was still touting their "Crestmark Body" to compete with GM's "Body By Fisher." The styling changes included a new grille with a bullet in place of the '52's "spinner," new chrome molding on the sides running along the rear fenders and a chrome handle mounted below the Ford Crest on the rear deck lid. The parking lights were changed from a circle format at the ends of the center grille to small horizontal lamps just under the grille bar.

Mainline, Customline and Crestline Series

Mainline, the basic Ford series, had both Tudor and Fordor sedans, a 3-passenger Business Coupe and a 2-door Ranch Wagon. The Customline mid-level models came as Tudor and Fordor sedans, a Club Coupe and 4-door Country Sedan station wagon. The top-of-the-line Crestline series featured the Victoria, the Sunliner convertible and the Country Squire 4-door station wagon. Crestlines came only with V-8 power. A six or a V-8 was available in all others.

All Ford Mainline and Customline models could be bought with a variety of seat cover materials, including All-Star rayon, Premier nylon, Candy Stripe plastic, Twill Tone fiber, Parade plastic, Fiesta fiber, Sportsman plastic, Check-weave fiber and Pastel Plaid plastic. These described different colors and patterns of the different materials available. All 1953 Ford seat covers had a rubber cable "quick-on" method of attachment. The covers could be attached with no rings, pins or zippers and helped give a good, tight fit and easy replacement.

Although chrome bumper and grille guards were popular add-ons in 1953, one of the more popular options was the exterior sun visor. It mounted just over the windshield and was designed to keep rain, snow and ice off of the windshield.

Ford and Chevy kept their pricing very close to each other on all comparable models. Chevy pegged their advertised prices slightly lower in almost all instances, but Ford offered both a six and a V-8 in most of its models. A Chevy Bel Air hardtop was $2,052, the Ford Victoria (with V-8) was $1,940 and the Plymouth Cranbrook was $2,064. The Chevrolet six-cylinder produced 108 horsepower in all models, while the Ford six stood at 101 horsepower and the V-8 at 110 horsepower. The Plymouth was still using the six-cylinder L-head engine with 100 horsepower.

The Victoria was still the cream of the crop when it came to style. It rounded out the style trio with the Country Squire and the Sunliner. The Crestline series came standard with a V-8 engine. (Photo: Henry Ford Museum and Ford Motor Company)

Coronado kits were all looks. The full-size spare in the trunk took up a good portion of the available luggage space. Fuel filler access was accessible from behind the license plate.

There were two cars prepared for the race and both had special chrome wire wheels. The dealer models looked the same but came with chrome wheel covers due to the high cost of the wires. The vehicle young Ford drove is still in the Henry Ford Museum and the second, backup car is now in the hands of a Southeastern Michigan collector.

1953 Sunliner
Indianapolis 500 Pace Car

Aside from hand painted Indy signage, one other tell-tale item unique to the actual pace cars was the AAA emblem (sanctioning body for the Indy 500 in 1953) shown on the Coronado deck kit.

The horn button at the center of the steering wheel had the 50th anniversary crest featured on all Fords that year. The interior was stock functionally and featured a special gold anniversary color scheme on the dash and upholstery.

Along with the special chrome wire wheels, the pace cars sported a Ford crest and crossed checkered flags on each front fender.

Spotlights with exterior mirrors were mounted to the A-pillars more for a more balanced, racy look than practicality.

Fender skirts were an option on the Sunliners but added to both the pace cars. The 1953 trim included stainless steel pieces on the rear fender bulge on all Crestliners.

Celebrating Ford's 50th year, Indianapolis Motor Speedway chose the Sunliner convertible as the pace car for the Memorial Day 500-mile event. Henry II's youngest brother, William Clay Ford, had received his promotion to a company vice president early in the month on May 12 and would now get to drive the pace car for the 37th Indy 500 with three-time Indy winner and raceway president Wilbur Shaw beside him. It must have been quite a month for young Bill Ford. He presented the keys to the pace car to race winner Bill Vukovich at the victory dinner that night.

The Ford boys were not new to the Indy track, because their father, Edsel Ford, had driven a Lincoln to pace the field in 1932 and then Henry "the deuce" drove a V-12 Lincoln in 1946. After William Clay's drive in the '53 Sunliner, the youngest brother, Benson, piloted a Mercury pace car the following year, 1954.

The William Clay-driven Ford Sunliner was one of the first recorded company pace car promotions. Ford built two vehicles with chrome wire wheels for the actual event and more than 2,000 replica vehicles to sell at dealerships.

The dealer lookalike vehicles all had chrome wheel covers instead of the wire versions on the pace cars. They were so popular that dealers started making replicas of the replicas to sell.

The pace cars were both painted "pace car white" with a matching top made from Orlon. The interior was "anniversary gold" including the dashboard and vinyl upholstery, and the special-built chrome wire wheels were mounted with Firestone tires.

Power for the Sunliner pace car came from the last of the 239 cubic-inch flathead V-8s. It had a Holley 2-barrel carburetor, 7.2:1 compression and produced the stock 110 horsepower. A stock 1953 Crestline Sunliner sold new for $2,042.

On May 12, 1953 William Clay Ford became a Ford vice president and later that month he and three-time Indy winner Wilbur Shaw paced the Indy 500 field in a new Sunliner. The convertible was the first pace car to have duplicates made, 2,000 of them, for sale at dealers across the country.

The graceful Sunliner had it all—a good-looking body design, whitewall tires, lots of chrome, a neatly stowed rag top and leather interior. (Photo: Henry Ford Museum and Ford Motor Company)

Taxicabs

Because Ford was marketing its products as low cost, durable vehicles, taxicabs were a natural target for sales. The modified, smoother suspension was a big selling point for the 1953 Fords and the company was pitching it as "a superb new ride and trend-setting style." The three major sales points were low initial cost, superior design, materials and workmanship and good resale—values a cab company would certainly put at the top of its list.

The taxi-specification Fords came with special seats with heavy-gauge springs in the cushions and in the seat backs. These were covered with firm foam rubber and optional vinyl seat covers that could be easily washed after heavy use.

Taxis were equipped with a heavy-duty 10-inch clutch for the expected 24-hour shifts and hard use. Ford Motor Company also showed front seat layouts in their advertising with two buckets seats—one facing forward for the driver and another facing rearward, toward the back seat passengers. Other options for taxis were heavy-duty generators, radiators, batteries and suspensions. Ford dealers offered one-quart fire extinguishers, spotlights, turn indicators, backup lights, glare-proof inside rear-view mirror and tinted safety glass.

Engineering Changes

Carryover Engines; Suspension Changes

The Ford engine lineup for 1953 was carried over unchanged from the previous year, featuring again the flathead Strato-Star V-8 and the Mileage Maker overhead-valve six. The 101-horsepower six was standard in the Mainline and Customline series, with the V-8 offered as an option. The V-8 was standard in the top-of-the-line Crestline series. A choice of automatic or manual transmission, with or without an overdrive option, was still available with either engine. Fiberglass insulation was added under the hood to help suppress engine compartment noise and keep engine heat from aging the paint on the hood.

One of the biggest changes was in the suspension of the '53 Ford. The 1952 model suspension was criticized for bottoming out in sharp dips and potholes. So the engineers added more travel to the front suspension, along with a skid plate to protect the oil pan. They also recalibrated the shock absorbers to give higher compression damping and better rebound control. Ford claimed an 80-percent reduction in road shock and doubled the front suspension travel. The rear springs now used one-piece woven fabric inserts (replacing previous two-piece inserts) to provide a bigger damping surface. Ford, the last major manufacturer in 1952 to use 16-inch wheels, made the switch to 15-inch wheels and tires as standard for the 1953 lineup.

With very basic aerodynamics, fuel metering and ignition systems, gas mileage for vehicles of this time period wasn't exactly what it is today. The following chart outlines mileage observed in a *Motor Trend* test of a 1953 Ford V-8 sedan with Fordomatic transmission and overdrive.

Mileage Chart—1953

Speed	Mileage
30 miles per hour	21.1 miles per gallon
45 miles per hour	19.1 miles per gallon
60 miles per hour	15.9 miles per gallon
75 miles per hour	12.8 miles per gallon

The Mainline Tudor sold for $1567 with a V-8 or $1496 with a six. Although a stripped model, it came with most of the same engineering standards as the more costly Crestlines. Ford produced 152,995 Mainline Tudors while 305,433 Customline Tudors rolled out the doors. (Photo: Henry Ford Museum and Ford Motor Company)

Under ideal conditions such as perfect tuning and professional driving, reasonably good mileage figures could be turned in. Ford was the victor in the Mobilgas Economy Run from Los Angeles to Sun Valley, Idaho, with a 1953 Ford Mainliner powered by the Mileage Maker Six engine. Driver Les Viland averaged 27 miles per gallon for the entire trip to win first place in Class A and the "Sweepstakes," the overall best mileage for the event. Hollywood Ford dealer Al Stuebing sponsored the winning Ford. Ford-built vehicles had dominated the event, with Lincoln winning in 1951 and Mercury in 1952.

Testing

In 1953, Ford had a cold room in its Dearborn testing facilities that could bring the temperature down to a chilly -60F/-51C when necessary. Most of the testing was done at a mere -20F/-28C, evaluating the ability of the vehicle to start in cold weather and function normally. The machinery used to chill the room was capable of turning out 600 tons of block ice per day.

1953 Ford vs. Chevy Comparison

	Ford	Chevrolet
Wheelbase	115"	115"
Overall length	198"	195.5"
Overall height	62"	63"
Overall width	73"	75"
Compression	7.0:1 6-cyl.	7.1:1 6-cyl.
	7.2:1 V-8	
Horsepower	101 6-cyl.	108 6-cyl.
	110 V-8	

1953 Model Car Pricing

	Six-cylinder	V-8
Mainline		
Business Coupe	$1399	$1470
Tudor Sedan	$1496	$1567
Fordor Sedan	$1541	$1612
Ranch Wagon	$1846	$1917
Customline		
Club Coupe	$1591	$1662
Tudor	$1582	$1652
Fordor	$1627	$1698
Country Sedan		$2076
Crestline		
Victoria		$1940
Sunliner Convertible		$2042
Country Squire		$2203

Prices include all taxes, oil filter, wiper booster, oil-bath air cleaner, electric clock, turn signals, license and title.

For 1953, Ford introduced an all-new series of pickups, panel trucks and medium and heavy duty trucks. This panel version of the F-100 was stylish and far superior in engineering and quality to the previous series F-1.

They're Here!

THE GREATEST LINE OF FORD TRUCKS EVER BUILT!

Availability of equipment, accessories and trim as illustrated is dependent on material supply conditions.

AMERICA'S NO. 1 ECONOMY FAVORITE— the Ford F-100 Pickup—has new 6½-ft. pickup box with new, rigid, clamp-tight tailgate.

"Fifty Years Forward on the American Road!"

Completely New for '53...
FORD *ECONOMY* TRUCKS

Ford trucks were all new for 1953. The cars, now in their second year of the new series, had only mild changes, so the company pushed truck advertising more in this anniversary year than it normally would have. The overhead-valve Cost Clipper six-cylinder (in its second year) and the newly added Fordomatic transmission were featured to bring the pickups closer to a dual purpose vehicle—car and truck.

1953 Factory Installed Accessories and Prices

Fordomatic	$189.52
Overdrive	112.99
6-tube radio	90.13
8-tube radio	102.49
Wiper booster	9.36
Leather trim	31.45
Tinted glass	23.82
Forced air heater	73.57
Recirculating air heater	45.21
Electric clock	15.14
Turn signals	15.72
Windshield washer	9.88
Undercoating	20.30
Outside sun visor	28.67
Fender skirts	24.00
Whitewall Tires	26.70

1953 Dealer Installed Accessories and Prices

Cigar lighter	$4.33
Clock (stem wind)	20.43
Rocker panel molding	17.78
Window vent shades (Tudor & Coupe)	18.37
Window vent shades (Fordor)	20.87
Wheel trim rings	13.09
Glare-proof mirror	5.07
Side cowl mirror	6.95
Side mirror (clamp)	3.60
Bumper guard (front)	29.99
Bumper guard (rear)	29.99
Chrome wheel discs	15.80
White wheel discs	15.80
Spotlight & mirror	27.18
Spotlight	26.46
Glove compartment light	3.45
Luggage compartment light	3.25
Backup light (right)	6.57
Backup light (left)	10.33
Backup light (left—Fordomatic)	8.27
Handbrake signal	5.80
Map light (Customline)	6.82
Engine compartment light	3.25

Completely New Ford Truck Lineup

Nineteen fifty-three was a significant year for Ford in the truck market. With little change in the cars, Ford needed something completely new to introduce in its 50th anniversary year. The new bodies and engineering on the trucks were a substantial change and the buying public was ready for the fresh and exciting look. With the F-100 models, Ford trucks were now more focused on style and driver comfort than ever before. In the past Ford expected its trucks to be used as a commercial tool, and there was no serious consideration given for comfort of the driver and passenger until the unveiling of the 1948 F-1 models. This was a big step, but the 1953 F-100 was a significant leap forward in driver consideration.

Investing more than $50 million in research, development and engineering, Ford was eager to present the stylish new F-100 truck line. By 1953, Ford had produced more than 17 million commercial vehicles in the United States alone and claimed to have placed all of its experience and know-how into the new models.

Designing a new truck often took years. With cars, Ford would build many different bodies to fit on a single chassis, but with trucks they built one body to fit on numerous chassis. A design would start with designers' sketches and engineers' calculations. From there it would move into clay models, blueprints, engine specifications, profiles and final master body drafts. Small 1/20th scale models were made first, then a 1/4 scale model of the best design. Once a number of executives had seen the 1/4 scale and approved, the clay modelers would start on the full-scale design for review.

The sleek 1953 Ford F-series trucks all had a "driverized cab" built with the driver in mind.

The smooth lines of the 1953 series became one of the all-time great truck body designs. With the torque of a V-8 engine, it was a snappy performer.

For 1953, the Ford pickups and panel trucks all featured the new F-100 logos, identifying them as an all-new generation of stylish, tough Ford trucks.

The interior of the panel truck was rather plain compared to the cars, but far more comfortable than drivers were used to. Spotlight handles intruded into the cab, but could be useful in a commercial vehicle.

Half-ton model trucks, the F-100s, could be bought with a Fordomatic transmission for the first time. Ford also offered two 3-speed transmissions and a 4-speed. One 3-speed was for the lighter F-100 and the other one was for the heavier F-250 and F-350 models. Previously saddled with flat windshields, the new trucks came with a beautiful wrap-around piece of glass that provided some 55 percent more viewing area than before.

The smooth lines of the 1953 series became one of the all-time great truck body designs. With the torque of a V-8 engine, it was a snappy performer, especially in an F-100 pickup. The pickups usually were sold with black-wall tires, but some owners chose to add whitewalls after the first set wore out.

This Mainline Fordor was typical of the Detroit Police car fleet in 1953. The V-8 powered sedans came with a light/siren combination on the forward roof and a Police sign on the hood for identification when pulling alongside other vehicles. (Photo: Henry Ford Museum and Ford Motor Company)

They had vastly improved seat comfort to reduce fatigue and help the driver get the job done easier and quicker. The cabs now had wide seats with lots of legroom and wide rear windows. The one-piece curved windshield had 55 percent more visibility and a modern look.

The popular light-duty F-100 model was now available with Fordomatic, the first automatic transmission offered in a Ford truck. Even though this was a novel idea for a truck of any sort, Fordomatic caught on quickly, becoming a popular option in the F-100. Automatic overdrive was also available as an option. The manual-shift transmissions now were of Ford's "Synchro-silent"

The Ford Courier, a model name to be used for the next 45 years on other vehicles, was listed as a truck although on a car chassis. The half-ton vehicle was used for light duty commercial businesses. (Photo: Henry Ford Museum and Ford Motor Company)

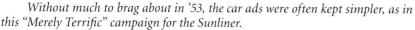

Without much to brag about in '53, the car ads were often kept simpler, as in this "Merely Terrific" campaign for the Sunliner.

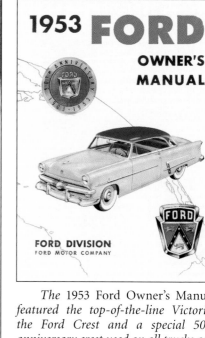

The 1953 Ford Owner's Manual featured the top-of-the-line Victoria, the Ford Crest and a special 50th anniversary crest used on all trucks and cars for that model year.

Ford found many ways to celebrate the fiftieth anniversary, with emblems on vehicles, special books and company communications. A rare copy of the magazine Clues, a truck oriented publication for dealers and their customers, features the brothers Ford—left to right: Benson, Henry and Bill.

design, cutting out much of the whining gear noise and incorporating a synchronized second gear for downshifting.

Five engines were now offered, including three V-8s and two six-cylinders throughout the lineup. The inline six for the most popular line, the F-Series, was a 215 cubic-inch displacement (CID) OHV model producing 101 horsepower and dubbed the Mileage Maker. The six-cylinder F-100 was priced at $1,012. The optional V-8 was still a flathead, or L-style, 239-CID engine with 106 horsepower.

The new F-Series trucks were produced at 15 Ford manufacturing plants across North America. The heavy-duty lines were only produced at Highland Park, Michigan.

▶

The 1954 Ford trucks all had a similar look with the major styling change in the bulky grille. The rest of the body looked basically the same as previous models, but now the F-100 series also came with an overhead-valve Y-block V-8. (Photo: Henry Ford Museum and Ford Motor Company)

FORD

The Year 1954

Exterior changes on the '54 models included a new grille and parking lights, new bumpers, headlight bezels and fresh taillights. The amber fog lamps were more often used for dressing up the car than actually used in the fog.

In 1954, the big news was Ford's overhead-valve V-8 engine, which had been in the design process for six years. This Harold Youngren design replaced the 22-year-old L-head, or flathead V-8. The six-cylinder had been upgraded the year before. Engineering also enlarged the inline six-cylinder and both engines were available in all models. Youngren had worked on the Oldsmobile overhead-valve V-8s before coming to Ford and knew the value of a full lineup of modern engines if the company was to be competitive in the future.

A MacPherson-designed ball-joint style front suspension was introduced in the Lincoln lineup two years prior and was now standard in the Fords, adding to ease of steering and a better ride. Model changes included a new 4-door sedan, the Skyliner hardtop with a Plexiglas half-roof and a 2-door station wagon. Exterior changes featured a new grille and parking lights, bumpers, headlight surrounds and new taillights. One unusual addition to the Sunliner convertible mentioned in early advertising was a clear plastic insert in the soft top over the front seat area to provide more light in the interior. The convertible top was power-operated and fit into a boot behind the rear seat.

Ford was the first manufacturer to install a plastic bag reservoir under the hood for holding windshield cleaner fluid. Until then, all manufacturers used glass containers that could easily freeze and crack during winter months.

By 1954, customers were starting to enjoy more convenient methods of driving. Thirty percent of the buyers chose Fordomatic, and another five percent purchased their cars with Ford's new power steering option.

Products

The last of a 3-year body design, the 1954 models looked similar to its predecessors with minor detail changes. The grille now incorporated a center spinner and small spinners housed the parking lights on either side. Both the Customline and Crestline series had a full-length chrome-molding strip down the side of the vehicle.

Mainline

The Mainline models were the base series and provided around 235,000 of the 1.16 million cars Ford produced in 1954. It lacked the chrome trim of the two upper model lines, but provided value at a base price of $1,542 for a Fordor sedan. The Mainline was available with most of the Ford options that year, but came standard with one sun visor, a horn button and only a driver-side armrest.

Customline

The Customline series was the midrange Ford and came standard with much more chrome. It could be had with almost all the options available on a Crestline model and accounted for the biggest chunk of production at Ford Motor Company that year. The Fordor and Tudor alone totaled well over a half million units in sales. Tudors provided hand straps to help rear passengers exit the vehicle, dual sun visors, armrests and extra chrome trim on the exterior.

Crestline

The big news for the Crestline series was the Victoria model with a transparent top. This had been shown only on concept cars at auto shows to that point. The Skyliner top was made of Plexiglas and looked great—but it could be hot in the summer with the sun bearing down. Print advertising in magazines claimed the dark-green tinted glass filtered out 60 percent of the sun's rays. Fortunately, Ford provided a curtain beneath the glass top to block out the sun when needed. The transparent Skyliner top covered the front half of the interior. Only 13,344 Skyliners were produced in '54.

Sunliner

The Sunliner convertible now had new nonfading, nonshrinking tops in four colors. The clear vinyl rear window could be zipped out and dropped into the boot area for extra ventilation in warm weather. Three weather-tight zippers were used to seal the window back in place. Pulling a button at the left of the steering column started the electro-hydraulic system to lower the top into the area behind the rear seat. Interiors were made up of two-tone pleated vinyl upholstery over foam rubber padded seats.

Station Wagons

The Ford station wagon model was a better handling vehicle than most other American wagons on the road. Several magazine articles in 1954 commented on the maneuverability of the Ford compared to GM and Chrysler wagons. It came out the winner in a *Motor Trend* test with comments such as, "I'm competition car-minded and have a wife and two kids. What more could I ask in a family car? This car can out handle some of the imports." Ford still generally got lower marks

on fit and finish, and after it had some miles on it, often received complaints of rattles. Final inspection at the assembly plants was not yet a fine art at Ford, but was getting much better. Chevrolet often got better marks on the fit and finish of the interior, but Ford was the performer.

Interior

The transparent back "Astra-Dial" speedometer allowed sunlight to illuminate the numbers and needle from behind. The high position on top of the dash made it easy to read the speed, but the transparent back sometimes caused sunlight to reflect onto the windshield, causing a distracting rainbow effect. This year saw red warning lights replace the amperage and oil-pressure gauges—a production economy move.

Interior changes included more color choices this year, and plastic upholstery was available on all models except the top-end Crestline models.

Trucks

For 1954, the F-100 pickup trucks could be equipped with the all-new 130-horsepower overhead-valve V-8, a $100 option. The standard OHV six-cylinder had been enlarged from 215 cubic inches to 223 and was dubbed the Cost Cutter Six. Ford sold more than 302,000 trucks in '54, of which 117,587 were the popular F-100 pickups.

Styling changes were few, having been redesigned the year before, but a new, bulky-looking grille was added along with slightly different badges on the sides of the hood.

The Skyliner came with specific instructions on how to care for the Plexiglas half top. Instructions in the owner's manual said to never wipe dust or dirt off the top with a dry cloth. Cleaning oil or grease off the top could be done by using a soft cloth and kerosene. (Photo: Henry Ford Museum and Ford Motor Company)

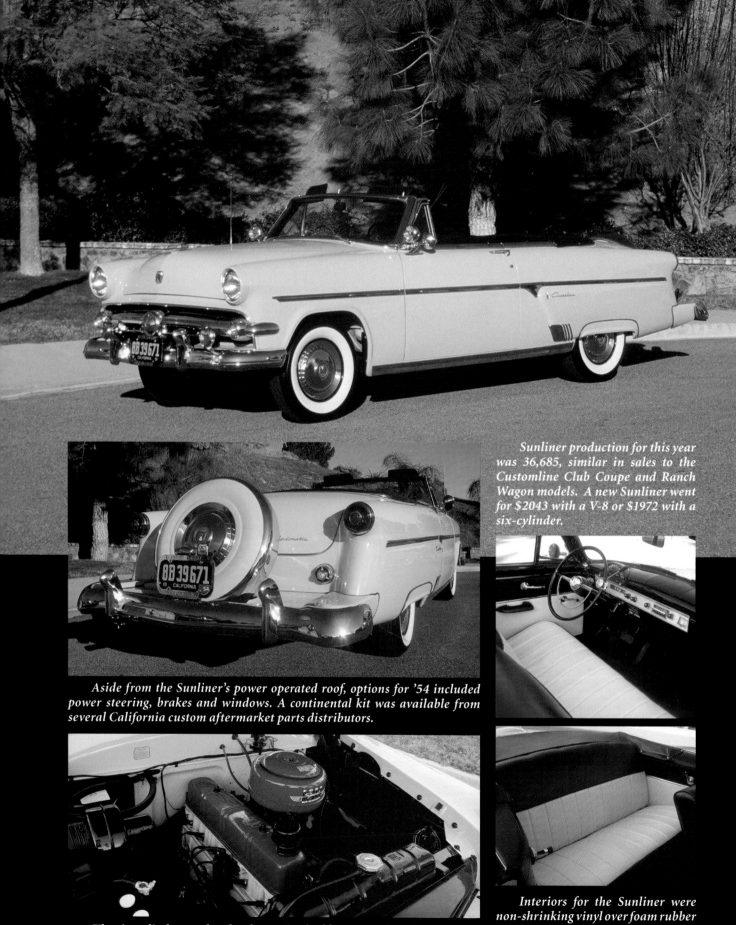

Sunliner production for this year was 36,685, similar in sales to the Customline Club Coupe and Ranch Wagon models. A new Sunliner went for $2043 with a V-8 or $1972 with a six-cylinder.

Aside from the Sunliner's power operated roof, options for '54 included power steering, brakes and windows. A continental kit was available from several California custom aftermarket parts distributors.

The six-cylinder overhead-valve engine had been introduced with the '52 model. It had sold well because it provided almost the same performance as the earlier flathead V-8, but now it lagged behind the all new overhead-valve

Interiors for the Sunliner were non-shrinking vinyl over foam rubber padding, available in four colors. The transparent vinyl rear window had three weather-tight zippers sealing it

Engineering Changes

Ford's New Overhead-Valve "Y-Block" V-8

The big news for 1954 was the 130-horsepower overhead-valve V-8 engine, the first in Ford history. Displacing 239 cubic inches (and no relation to the 239 CID flathead V-8), the all-new OHV V-8 provided 21 more foot-pounds of torque and 15 extra horsepower than the refined version of the Mileage Maker Six, which was now rated at 115 horsepower. In development since 1948, the new OHV V-8 would again keep Ford in the forefront of low-priced cars, a year ahead of Chevrolet's first V-8.

Ford engineers had several goals in mind when designing the new line of engines. They wanted to keep approximately the same weight, overall size and displacement as the flathead V-8.

Master Glide power steering was available in all models. It cut the steering effort by 75 percent, according to Ford. The company claimed that "while on the straightaway," the steering would retain its natural feel, but it took all the effort out of parking. (Photo: Dan Kaiser)

Ford recommended that the "break-in" lubricants be changed after 300 miles. The car was later to be returned to the dealer for a 1,000 mile inspection and engine oil was changed every 2,000 miles. (Photo: Henry Ford Museum and Ford Motor Company)

The Victoria featured a full length chrome strip down each side along with a chrome protection piece on the rear fender bulge. Rear windows rolled completely out of sight for a clean, open air look. (Photo: Henry Ford Museum and Ford Motor Company)

The Country Squire wagon was still the cream of the crop when it came to family transportation. (Photo: Henry Ford Museum and Ford Motor Company)

1954 Model Car Pricing

	Six-cylinder	V-8
Mainline		
Business Coupe	$1400	$1471
Tudor Sedan	$1496	$1567
Fordor Sedan	$1542	$1618
Ranch Wagon	$1846	$1917
Customline		
Tudor Sedan	$1582	$1653
Fordor Sedan	$1628	$1699
Club Coupe	$1591	$1662
Ranch Wagon	$1932	$2003
Country Sedan Wagon	$2006	$2077
Crestline		
Fordor	$1726	$1797
Victoria	$1870	$1941
Sunliner convertible	$1972	$2043
Skyliner	$1972	$2043
Country Squire Wagon	$2132	$2204

More than 640 experimental engines were developed by Ford in the development of the 130 horsepower Y-block V-8.

The tops, which stowed neatly behind the rear seat, came in black or three other colors. A plastic insert covering the front compartment was available at extra cost only with the black top.

A unique touch for the dealer introduction of the overhead-valve V-8 engines in '54 was a Plexiglas window in the hood for showroom viewing. The hood came from Ford with small lights mounted on the underside of the surface to illuminate the new engine.

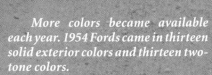

More colors became available each year. 1954 Fords came in thirteen solid exterior colors and thirteen two-tone colors.

Ford offered a four-way power front seat for the first time in 1954. The $64.50 option allowed 1 3/4 inches of vertical motion and 4 1/2 inches of horizontal movement.

Other goals included a higher compression ratio, an overhead-valve arrangement, and a short-stroke, simple design to allow for more automation in the machining and assembly process. The new engine had a chain-driven camshaft, more horsepower than the old engines, a single water pump and plenty of torque. Nearly 600,000 man-hours and six years went into the development of the new series of 90-degree OHV V-8s.

The new V-8 block was a one-piece iron casting designed to be as rigid as possible for smoothness and approximately the same weight as the old L-head block. The engineers accomplished their goal of a short-stroke engine, overhead valves and maximum simplicity.

It provided much lower friction and better breathing than its predecessor and higher horsepower at the same displacement.

There were, however, a few hiccups. The new V-8's spark plugs were difficult to change, located under the exhaust manifold, and the oil filter was only accessible from underneath the vehicle.

1954 Ford Engines

	Six	V-8
Number of cylinders:	6	8
Type:	Inline overhead-valve	90° V overhead-valve
Bore (inches):	3.62	3.50
Stroke (inches):	3.60	3.10
Displacement (cubic inches):	223	239
Compression ratio:	7.2 to 1	7.2 to 1
Maximum bhp:	115 @ 3900	130 @ 4200
Maximum torque* (lb-ft):	193 @ 1000-2200	214 @ 1800-2200
Bhp per cu. in. displacement:	0.516	0.544

*Bhp and torque corrected to 60F dry air at 29.92 in. of mercury

This Victoria came with the optional full wheel covers and whitewall tires. The V-8 in a Victoria was optional, but came in a majority of the cars. (Photo: Henry Ford Museum and Ford Motor Company)

The last year of Walker's second generation of Fords was not widely different than the 1952 models, but the car was certainly the most refined of the three. The brakes, suspension and the new Y-block overhead-valve V-8 were all far superior to the earlier models.

The freshened grille was one of the few obvious changes to the exterior in '54. Better designed shocks helped for better rebound control on rough roads.

Aside from the Sunliner's power-operated roof, options for '54 included power steering, brakes and windows.

The Sunliner top was supposed to be washed with FoMoCo Foam Upholstery Cleaner or a mild soap every three months at minimum. Ford also offered top dye through its dealers to restore the original color to a faded top. (Photo: Henry Ford Museum and Ford Motor Company)

A Ford with the new V-8 could accelerate to 60 in 17.2 seconds and top speed runs averaged 87 miles per hour. The speedometer read "65" when at a true 60 miles per hour according to Motor Trend *magazine.*

Some of the early-production engines had problems with cam lobe wear. Because the new engines were produced and stockpiled ahead of production of the new model cars, a car produced some weeks after the production start date could still end up with a faulty cam lobe, but Ford repaired these problems free of charge.

Motor Trend magazine editors liked the new Ford, especially the new V-8 and the ball-joint front suspension. Even though there was little difference in the body, the performance under the hood and in the suspension impressed them. The car accelerated from zero to 60 mph in 17.2 seconds and top speed was 89.9 mph. Although Ford skipped hydraulic valve lifters in favor of the more economical mechanical tappets, the engine was still quiet enough to earn high marks from the staff. "Manufacturing cost may be a factor here. However, we feel that the '54 engine is adequately quiet without hydraulic lifters, a tribute to its design." The fuel consumption for the new V-8 at a steady 60 mph was 14.9 mpg. This dropped to 11.9 mpg at 75 mph.

New Fords await shipment outside their birthplace at the famous Rouge Assembly Plant. Notice the black Sunliner with protective plastic over the new soft top. (Photo: Henry Ford Museum and Ford Motor Company)

The Rouge Facility

The Rouge Plant, which opened in 1920, was known in the 1950s as the world's largest industrial city. It covered 1,200 acres, employed more than 63,000 people and boasted a complete recreation program for "after-hours relaxation for employees. Technical schools give classroom and on-the-job training looking to the constant advancement of employees," according to one visitor's brochure.

The Rouge housed blast furnaces, shipping docks, assembly lines, machine shops, a glass plant and coke ovens for making steel products. Raw materials would roll into one end of the Rouge while finished products rolled out the other. The Rouge built vehicles for distribution in Michigan but also manufactured parts to be shipped to Ford plants all over the country. More than a half-billion gallons of water were used each day to keep the Rouge running.

- Average daily payroll in 1954: $1,250,000
- Total square footage of Rouge buildings: 15,800,000 square feet
- One hundred miles of conveyers
- More than 110 miles of railroad within the plant acreage
- Ships brought in approximately 1.6 million tons of ore and 2.3 million tons of coal annually
- A medical staff of 175, including 12 doctors and 32 nurses

The six passenger Crestline Victoria along with the rest of the 1954 Ford cars now used a ball joint front suspension, replacing the older type king pin system. This provided up and down movement of the front wheels along with direction movement under hard cornering.

New Suspension

The new ball-joint front suspension on the '54 Ford made the difference in handling over the previous models. *Motor Trend* writer Jim Potter said, "We found that the car had the best stability on sharp turns of any car in its price class." But they also felt that

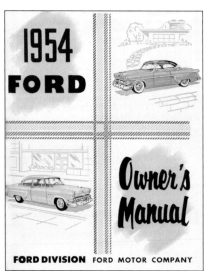

The owner's manual for 1954 pictured cars from the top and bottom of the line. At the bottom was the Mainline Tudor, which accounted for 123,329 units of Ford production that year. The Victoria production was only 95,464 but was far more profitable.

at low speeds that Ford wasn't quite as easy to steer as some of its competition. This was a modified version of the front suspension introduced in the 1952 model Lincoln.

The Ford was well sprung with five-leaf rear springs and rubber bushings between the ends of each leaf to keep them quiet. The ride for a low-priced vehicle was considered excellent, handling bumps, ruts and railroad tracks with ease.

The brakes were much improved, stopping from 60 mph 13 feet shorter than the 1953 models. Stronger brake mounts and heavier shoes helped accomplished this.

Power Options

It was the year of the power options and Ford now offered power-lift windows, four-way power seats, power steering and power brakes.

The Fordomatic and overdrive options were still available in all models and becoming very popular as the percentage of cars sold with automatic transmissions continued to grow.

1954 Accessories

	Price
Fordomatic Drive	$184
Overdrive	$110
Master Guide power steering	$134
Swift-Sure power brakes	$41
Power-lift windows	$102
Power seat	$64
Whitewall tires (exchange)	$27

Another interesting cost breakdown was for parts that often needed to be replaced on a typical automobile and the labor charges at a Ford dealer. The charges were a bit more reasonable during the mid-'50s than they are today.

Ford Part	Customer Price	Dealer Labor Charge
Distributor	$12.85	$1.40
Battery	$18.95	$0.70
Fuel pump	$5.64	$1.75
Valve grind	$2.40	$38.15
Front fender	$28.12	$12.25
Bumper	$30.53	$2.80

▶

Cal Beauregard from Ford's New York marketing and sales office drove the all-new Thunderbird in New York City's 1954 Columbus Day Parade. (Photo: Cal Beauregard collection)

FORD

The 'Bird was only 5 1/2 inches off the street, much lower than the sedans. A three speed manual was standard and the Fordomatic was optional, a choice made by the majority of the buyers.

The Year 1955

All-new Models for '55

A year of new models, 1955 saw more great body styles, including the new Thunderbird under the design direction of George Walker.

Walker, who had designed the '49 to '51 and '52 to '54 model series as a consultant to Ford, was named a company vice president in 1955, giving the Ford design team much deserved clout within the company. He reported to L.D. Crusoe, then an executive vice president in charge of car and truck divisions.

Another notable management change was the promotion of Ernie Breech to the newly created position of Chairman of the Board of Directors—Ford Motor Company's first chairman.

Of the remaining seven "Whiz Kids," Robert McNamara was moved up in position to vice president of Ford Division.

Sales for 1955 were outstanding—a new Ford record—and they closed within touching distance of Chevrolet. Only a handful of vehicles kept them out of the number-one position. Regaining the sales lead from Chevy had been one of Henry II's goals since he took charge of the company. The "Beat Chevy" theme from 1949 was still ringing in the ears of the world's second largest division, and they could see victory in sight.

Products

Another All-New Ford Lineup

Ford introduced four model lines at 6,400 Ford dealers across the country on November 12, 1954. With the all-new Fairlane models, the company once again added a new high-end line with stylish trim packages and options, demoting the Customline and Mainline models a notch. The Station Wagon line had its own top and bottom series ranging from the Country Squire on down to the Custom Ranch Wagon.

All models had a wraparound windshield and a lower profile. The Crown Victoria made its debut with the famous non-structural chrome band across the roof. Still in the lineup was a Skyliner model, with a chrome band and a Plexiglas half-roof over the front seat, the sexy-looking style leader for the new Ford lineup.

Ford marketing decided something akin to GM's "Body By Fisher" moniker was needed to tell the public that Ford's car bodies were built with quality. In 1952, Ford had introduced the Coachcraft body to differentiate it from the dismal '49 body. So someone at Ford came up with a new name for the '53 lineup, "Ford Crestmark Bodies," to describe the next-generation designs. The name really never caught on and was gradually dropped. The Fisher name seemed to work for GM because the bodies were literally designed and produced by Fisher Body, a specialist in the industry.

Fairlane

Fairlane and Fairlane Victoria models entered the Ford lineup in 1955 with a full complement of new body styles and engine combinations. All Fairlanes and Victorias carried the striking V-shaped chrome side trim, chrome headlight trim, full wheel covers and hardtop styling without B-pillars (the Crown band was non-structural). The Fairlane

Town and Club Sedans, which did have B-pillars, had some of the trim of the Victorias, but a little less style. All Fairlane models came standard with fender skirts, separating them from all the other models. Ford worked to keep each line separated by levels of comfort and visual appeal. All models were built on a 115.5-inch wheelbase.

Customline

The second-tier Customline models included a Fordor and Tudor. Both were finished with the same trim and available options. The upholstery was patterned over foam rubber cushions and padded armrests were in place for front and rear passengers.

Customline models could be had with a six or V-8, Fordomatic, overdrive or manual 3-speed transmissions, and power options such as brakes, steering, windows and seats were available.

Mainline

The trusty Mainline series was for the entry-level buyer, the customer who needed all the size and mechanical soundness of a Ford, but without the fancy trim and accessories. These were fairly bland-looking next to a Fairlane, but actually did about the same job on the road and could be bought with many of the options available on the higher models.

Thunderbird

Ford's most exciting "flagship" news for the year came in the form of a beautiful two-seater described as a personal luxury car. The Thunderbird was an exciting answer to Chevrolet's Corvette, but even better because it had all the same flare combined with greater sales potential. The 'Vette never amounted to more than an excitement builder for Chevrolet, selling in volumes far lower than the Thunderbird.

Chase Morsey worked with Davis and Crusoe in laying out the personality of the Thunderbird. Engineering wanted to match what Chevrolet was doing with the Corvette, the American sports car, but marketing saw that the 1953–54 Corvette had a six-cylinder engine, a rock-hard suspension and nothing in the way of personal luxury accessories. Morsey wanted the T-Bird personality to be focused on personal luxury—a two-seater sports model with air conditioning, power windows, power brakes and a good ride. He wanted a cool-looking boulevard cruiser. "I didn't want it to be another Corvette," said Morsey. "I wanted something that would bring the customers into the showrooms, not just another Chevrolet lookalike."

The Thunderbird became just that—a great-looking cruising machine. It offered the customer all the comforts of a true luxury car, but with the sporty look of a two-seat sports car. Apparently it was the right combination and the correct decision, because 16,155 Thunderbirds were sold in its first year, compared to 674 for Corvette. It became an instant status symbol with Hollywood

stars, and the country was totally enamored with the good looks of the 'Bird. In its three classic years, 1955 to 1957, the Thunderbird sold more than 53,000 cars.

Numerous stories describe how the T-Bird got its name, but George Walker, in his interview with the Henry Ford Museum's Dave Crippen, made his version clear. ". . . Breech was joining the Thunderbird Club out in Palm Springs to play golf. He came back one day and said to Henry, 'If you can't think of a name, why don't you call it the Thunderbird?' Henry said, 'That's it.'"

L. D. Crusoe's personal Thunderbird sported Fairlane chrome trim, which showed up in early advertising but never hit production. This model also had a continental kit with extended exhaust exits, but all production '55 'Birds had a spare contained in the trunk. (Photo: Henry Ford Museum and Ford Motor Company)

There was limited trunk space in the Thunderbird due to a full-size spare mounted off to the right side of the area. The T-bird's trunk lid was counterbalanced and would pop up with a turn of the key.

The Thunderbird had what Ford called an Astra-Dial control panel including a tachometer and a clock with a sweep second hand.

Four-way power seats were standard on the Thunderbird and controlled from a set of switches mounted on the driver's door.

Early Ford advertising indicated that the all-new personal luxury car would come with a 160-horsepower V-8, but production saw a 193-horsepower V-8 with the manual transmission or a 198-horse V-8 with the automatic. A 4-barrel carburetor and dual exhausts were included with all Thunderbirds.

The '55 T-bird was a good-looking, tight package with a Ferrari-like grille, a clean slab side and fender skirts. The base price was $2695 and the fiberglass hardtop was standard with the soft folding top being an option.

6 a.m. THUNDERBIRD time

Doctor, Lawyer, Merchant, Chief—no matter who you are—you'll find yourself getting up early when your garage is home to a Thunderbird. For here is a truly delightful package of sheer pleasure—all the way from its "let's go" look to the "let's go" performance of its Thunderbird Special Y-block V-8. What's more—that seat is nearly *five feet* wide and it's power-operated. A touch of a switch moves it *up, down*—forward or back to suit your requirements for driving comfort. The steering wheel is

another comfort feature—adjust it as you like it.
As for weather—your Thunderbird can have an easily demountable hard top and/or a snug fabric top that folds away completely out of sight. Windows roll up . . . power-operated if you like. Power steering, power brakes, Overdrive and Speed-Trigger Fordomatic are also available. These are important details, but the main thing is the low and mighty car itself! Why don't you obey that urge and try one today? Your Ford Dealer is the man to see.

The Thunderbird is now available in 5 colors!

This is the Thunderbird Special Y-block V-8 4-barrel carburetor, 8.5 to 1 compression ratio, 198-h.p. with Fordomatic . . . try it!

An exciting original by FORD

A successful businessman is shown leaving for work in an affluent neighborhood at "6 a.m. Thunderbird time." The personal luxury theme ran throughout Ford print advertising.

At its public unveiling during the Detroit Auto Show on February 20, 1954, the product was described by Ford Division marketing as a personal car. "The Thunderbird will begin a new era in the automotive field," said Ford Division vice president L.D. Crusoe. "While it resembles a sports car, it is a full-size vehicle—most of the major parts are interchangeable with our regular line of cars. It is completely engineered and built so it can be serviced by any Ford dealer." And so the Thunderbird was launched with a much larger potential

buying audience in mind than Chevrolet's Corvette. Crusoe and Morsey had ensured that it was not considered competition to the 'Vette, and would appeal to upscale customers who could afford to buy it.

The New York introduction of the Thunderbird was in the Columbus Day Parade on October 12, 1954, although it had been officially introduced to the press the month before. People were asking, "What is a 'Thunderbird?'" because there were no Ford identification markings.
They were told it was a Ford.

In a stunning red, the T-Bird was the hit of the Columbus Day Parade that year. It was driven by Cal Beauregard from sales and Ford public relations man, John Cameron. "It was a brand-new car," said Cameron, "and cruising along at four or five miles per hour, it finally started overheating. Just as I got to the reviewing stand, the car died and there wasn't a thing I could do about it." Beauregard ran back to Cameron's car and helped him push it out of the way so the rest of the parade could get by. After a few minutes they got it started again and finished the parade, but not before being embarrassed in front of the crowd.

Early reports in employee publications and Ford advertising materials indicated the Thunderbird would be powered by a 160-horsepower, 256 cubic-inch engine equipped with a 4-barrel carburetor and dual exhausts. These ad materials also pictured the T-Bird with a 1954 license plate. The 160-horsepower 256 CID V-8 didn't provide enough power in the pre-production 'Bird, so production versions were upgraded to the 292 cubic-inch (same as the Mercury engine) Thunderbird Special V-8.

The manual-transmission versions had 193 horsepower and the Fordomatic came with 198 horses. The short-stroke "Trigger Torque" Y-block V-8 engine provided much better acceleration than the 272 cubic-inch engine in the sedans.

One advertisement quoted, "From a standing start, in 40 seconds the Thunderbird will be 53 car lengths out in front of a conventional 1954 car." It didn't say just what the "conventional car" was, but it did suggest that acceleration was good. The 3-speed manual transmission could be equipped with optional overdrive. Fordomatic had three forward gears with no overdrive available.

Road & Track magazine described the Thunderbird as "a touring-sports car, designed to give sports-car qualities up to a point, combined with enough comfort to satisfy the most delicate of constitutions. It is an extremely practical machine for personal transport over any distance in any kind of weather."

The writers found that with the 198-horsepower V-8 and Fordomatic, they could manage a 0-60 mph time of 9.5 seconds with forced shifting through the gears. The top speed was 112 mph even though the speedometer indicated an optimistic 125 mph.

A single bench seat was standard in the T-Bird, seating three across, and the steering wheel was adjustable to fit the driver. The windshield wrapped around in one piece of safety glass and the option list included power steering, brakes and windows.

The steering wheel would telescope three inches to fit the driver's reach. In the dash the speedometer was mounted high for easy viewing, flanked on the left by a 5,000-rpm tachometer and an equal-size clock to the right with a sweep second hand. The upholstery was all vinyl in white and the trim matched the body color.

The optional removable fiberglass hardtop weighed in at 65 pounds. It latched tightly in place for a good winterized seal and came in the same color as the body.

The folding soft top was standard and would fold down completely behind the seat backs. This left more space for luggage, but with the spare tire taking up the right half of the trunk, not much room was left.

Only 51.5 inches high, the Thunderbird weighed in at 2,837 pounds. The frame was an X-style configuration, and it shared the ball-joint front suspension with the sedans.

This early print ad prepared by J. Walter Thompson for Ford showed the Fairlane trim running the length of the vehicle. The chrome strips were dropped for production models, which gave it a cleaner look, but ultimately left it more vulnerable to parking lot dings.

The Thunderbird shared most mechanical parts with the Ford sedans including suspension, engine and many body trim parts.

This Fordomatic-equipped Fairlane Sunliner had exhaust extensions to clear the continental kit.

New full-circle heater, clock and radio controls were backlit for easy nighttime viewing.

The transparent hood over the speedometer, carried over from the '54 models, allowed daylight in to make the numbers more readable for the driver. Most road testers said they loved the position, up high where the driver could see the instrument, but they could do without the clear hood over it.

The Thunderbird V-8 option, 193 horsepower with the manual transmission, and 198 horsepower with Fordomatic.

The taillight lens was shared with the new Thunderbird and even the rear fenders were similar. Backup lights were inset in the top portion of the fin.

The foam rubber seat cushions were wrapped over non-sag springs. Upholstery was two-tone vinyl and washable with soapy water.

The famous "bumble bee" black and Goldenrod yellow paint scheme was used in numerous print advertisements for the Fairlane Sunliner. The Ford Crestmark body was wrapped around a host of mechanical improvements. The new bodies featured a wraparound windshield to provide 1,100 square inches of glass area. Ford now offered tinted green glass in all windows it dubbed I-REST.

Thunderbirds came standard with a telescoping steering wheel to accommodate different drivers and driving positions. This model had the 3-speed manual transmission and power brakes and steering. (Photo: Henry Ford Museum and Ford Motor Company)

Engineering Changes

There were big changes in both the new body styling and the mechanical end of the '55 models. The wraparound windshield came all the way back to the nearly vertical A-pillars, adding a more modern appearance and better visibility for the driver. The rear window was also a wraparound piece of glass and all windows could be had in the optional green-tinted "I-REST" safety glass.

The seats in Fairlane and Customline models were foam rubber supported by springs. The dashboard had the speedometer mounted high, and like the 1954 models, used the clear plastic back for daylight illumination. The dash was dubbed the Astra-Dial control panel and featured three large circular dials in the center for the temperature control, radio and clock. The glove box was to the right and on either side of the steering column were controls for the wipers, ignition, parking and headlamps as well as the lighter.

Engines for '55 were still basically the same design as the '54 model but grew by another 33 cubic inches. Although Ford increased the compression ratio,

Trucks

For the first time, Ford trucks had tubeless tires, and a Custom model now replaced the former top-of-the-line Deluxe series. The trucks didn't change appreciably from the 1953–54 models but Ford sold 152,916 F-100 models alone. The wheelbase was 110 inches on the pickup and engines included the Cost Clipper Six at 118 horsepower and the optional Power King V-8 at 132 horsepower.

A new grille, reverting to the '53 look that was much cleaner and appealing than the '54, differentiated this year's body style.

1955 Model Car Pricing		
	Six-cylinder	V-8
Mainline		
Tudor	$1558	$1651
Business Tudor	$1464	$1557
Fordor	$1601	$1694
Customline		
Tudor	$1645	$1738
Fordor	$1686	$1779
Fairlane		
Club Sedan	$1750	$1843
Town Sedan	$1793	$1886
Victoria	$1919	$2012
Crown Victoria		
(solid top)	$2019	$2112
Crown Victoria Skyliner		
(transparent top)	$2084	$2177
Sunliner convertible	$2039	$2132
Station Wagon series		
Ranch Wagon	$1870	$1963
Custom Ranch		
Wagon	$1931	$2024
Custom Sedan		
(6-passenger)	$1976	$2069
Custom Sedan		
(8-passenger)	$2098	$2191
Country Squire	$2195	$2288
Courier		
(panel delivery)	$1598	$1691
Thunderbird		
Thunderbird		$2695*

* Price included hardtop; soft top was optional. Hardtop could be deleted on order.

The new Fairlane Sunliner had a totally new look for Ford cars and the Goldenrod yellow and black two-tone combination was eye catching. Many of the ads suggested that if you bought a big Ford, you got Thunderbird styling in the deal. Of course, many of the parts were shared between the vehicles.

the '55 engines still ran on regular grade gas and used new anti-fouling spark plugs plus a new camshaft. The 2-barrel version was rated at 162 horses while the new, high-performance version with a 4-barrel produced 182 hp. The hotter version also came with increased compression (8.5:1), a beefier radiator and a high-performance intake manifold that called for high-octane fuel. The Thunderbird Special was a 292 cubic-inch engine with 193 horse-power with manual transmission, and 198 hp with the Fordomatic.

The six-cylinder OHV engine was boosted to 120 horsepower and a 7.5:1 compression ratio.

Plymouth was still using an L-head six at 117 horsepower and its V-8 lineup ranged from 157 to 177 horsepower. The latter was its 4-barrel version. Chevy's six-cylinder was an overhead-valve powerplant and rated from 123 to 136 horsepower. This was the big year for Chevy, introducing its first ever V-8, which weighed in at 30 pounds less than its six. It matched Ford's horsepower at 162 with an 8:1 compression ratio.

Designing the '55

In a 41-month process starting in May of 1951, marketing and sales management discussed what a 1955 model Ford sedan should be. They talked about what size exterior and interior it should have, what kind of engines and features customers would want three and a half years from then. By January, 1952, these details were sorted out and approved and the styling studio started work on the actual exterior and interior look for the new model. In August,

NANKIN – MILLS

The clean dash design for '55 was all new with the exception of the transparent-top speedometer. There was seating for three across. Seat belts would not come as an option until the following year.

Power assist options were now becoming prevalent in the second year of these options. Power seats, steering, brakes and windows were hardly in a majority of the sales just yet, but Ford pushed them heavily in their sales brochures.

Crown Victoria production was 33,165 compared with the standard Victoria model at 113,372. Only 1,999 Crown Victoria Skyliner glass-top models were produced.

The Ford V-8 engine options for 1955 included 162 and 182 horsepower "Trigger-Torque" versions. The base engine was the 120-horse inline six.

The trio of Magic Aire all-climate controls, the super range radio and the precision built-in clock were all lined up within easy reach of the driver and passengers.

The Ford V-8 grew by 33 cubic inches in '55 to 272, producing 162 horsepower. The Fairlane models with Fordomatic could be bought with a higher-compression four-barrel V-8 rated at 182 horsepower.

management had approved the basic exterior design and clay models were started while engineering worked on the mechanical tasks. By April, 1953, the wooden pattern models were finished for the toolmakers and the engine division moved ahead with engine combinations and performance goals. In September of '54, parts were being sent to dealers so they would be stocked to repair the new models from the day they were sold. By early October, 1954, the last '54 model came off the line, the plants were shut down for their changeover, and by the end of the same month, the new 1955 models were rolling down the line.

People Who Help Build New '55 Ford Model Cars Are First to View Them

In line with a longstanding company policy, employees previewed 1955 Ford models prior to their introduction to the public November 12.

Traditionally those who help to build company cars have had the first opportunity to view their finished product. The new models were on display at 14 locations at the Rouge.

Meanwhile, in anticipation of a highly competitive sales year, Henry Ford II sent a personal letter announcing the new cars to every man and woman working at plants across the nation.

Ford wrote that each Ford man or woman can increase personal security by personally recommending to friends and neighbors the purchase of the product the employee helps produce.

He emphasized, "the strength of our company depends upon how well our products sell."

The Radio Cab company was heavy into Fords in 1955. Ford worked hard to gain fleet sales such as these with advertising that focused on durability and long-term low cost maintenance. (Photo: Henry Ford Museum and Ford Motor Company)

The Big Three Engine Lineup for 1955

	cubic inches	horsepower
Ford six-cylinder	223	120
Ford V-8	272	162 or 182
Chevrolet six-cylinder	235	123 or 136
Chevrolet V-8	265	162
Plymouth six-cylinder	230	117
Plymouth V-8	241	157 or 167
Plymouth V-8	259	177

New Plants Open

Nineteen fifty-five ushered in three new assembly plants for Ford while the company closed three others. In January, Ford moved car and truck assembly from Richmond, California, to San Jose, 51 miles away. The Louisville Plant moved in April to a new site across town, and the Edgewater Plant in New Jersey would close down and move 26 miles to its new home in Mahwah during the summer. The Mahwah move was completed in four days, with the last car at the 25-year-old Edgewater plant coming off the line on a Thursday and production starting at the new site on the following Monday. Both highway and rail transport were used to move the equipment, which included tools, production materials and office equipment. The heavy machinery from the plant was moved by train. Most of the 2,700 employees transferred to the new plant.

Safety was Ford's theme in 1956, introducing the Lifeguard design to help protect occupants against major injury hazards. This included a deep-dish steering wheel, padded dash and sun visors and the most important introduction, seat belts available in all models. This public relations photo shows a child being secured into a new Thunderbird. (Photo: Ford Motor Company)

FORD

The Year 1956

Dealers carried Plexiglas replacement kits during the 1954–56 Skyliner period. The plastic tops scratched easily and sometimes needed to be replaced.

In 1956, sales slid in marked contrast to the booming market success for most auto manufacturers in 1955. First-quarter production for the industry was heavy in preparation for the usual spring sales upturn, but unfortunately, it didn't materialize and dealers had to discount heavily to sell off stock before the 1957 models arrived in September. Total U.S. car and truck production dropped from the 1955 record of more than 9 million units to 6.9 million in '56.

Ford sales were still marginal, but by October, 1956 Benson Ford urged all dealers to start ordering because the company had boosted production by approximately 60 percent. He said that with the all-new Fords for '57, dealers would need to keep stock on hand. Plus, Ford hoped finally to outsell Chevrolet with its new model lineup.

Special options that used to be sold only in a small percentage of automobiles were now accounting for a major percentage of the manufacturers' income. Automatic transmissions now enjoyed 74 percent of the car market, power steering was found in one of every four cars, and power brakes were now installed in 24 percent of new cars sold. New body styles were finding favor too. The sporty hardtop design now comprised 31 percent of the total car market, while station wagons were the choice in 11 percent of sales.

The product lineup was a refinement of the 1955 series with changes in the parking lights, side trim and grille.

Ford expanded its Dearborn test track facilities with a laboratory for carburetor and fuel-injection testing. It constructed a huge wind tunnel for testing cooling, heating, air conditioning and aerodynamic properties of new body designs. Plus Ford opened the gates to the new Romeo Proving Ground test facility covering 3,880 acres north of Detroit.

Ford started teasing the public with mention of the first details about "Car E," a code name for the coming Edsel. It would be entered in the medium-price field, according to news releases promoting the first really new model in the industry in 20 years.

Lee Iacocca was an assistant sales manager for the Philadelphia district from 1953–56. When Ford's '56 lineup focused on a new safety package with seat belts and a padded dash, the company sent videos to all district sales offices to help the sales force promote the new image of Ford cars. Young Iacocca put his name in front of the giants in Dearborn by putting together a unique sales package promotion. He marketed a Custom Tudor with special two-tone paint, whitewall tires, radio and a heater that the masses could afford. If they put 20 percent down, they could have this new '56 Ford for $56 per month for 36 months. This promotion, "'56 for $56," caught Robert McNamara's attention when the Philadelphia region went from last to first place in sales nationwide in a 3-month period. It also earned Iacocca a promotion to district manager of the Washington, D.C., region. Later that year, the program was taken nationwide and it was estimated that the company sold an additional 75,000 Ford special models. Later that year, Iacocca was promoted to truck marketing manager back in Dearborn.

Robert McNamara, one of the original Whiz Kids and one of the brightest, was still the head of Ford Division. He had begun plans to build Ford's first small car by 1960, the Falcon. Ford Motor Company had studied the potential of a small car since the late 1940s, but the board had always turned down proposals, saying that the Henry J, Allstate and Metropolitan had all been no more than curiosities. But this time it appeared that all the major manufacturers were planning small cars and Ford would be there too.

Big Stock Sale

In 1903, Henry Ford sold 1,000 shares of Ford stock at $100 each. If you had purchased only one of those initial shares, by 1913 it would have been worth $190,000. Fifty-three years after the initial offer of stock, Ford Motor Company issued 10.2 million shares of common stock to the buying public through the New York Stock Exchange, raising $657 million at $64.50 per share. This was the equivalent of more than 20 percent of the company. The net proceeds, totaling $642 million, were given to the Ford Foundation, the philanthropy started by the Ford family to support U.S. education and many other good causes. Almost all of the 250,000 buyers of the stock purchased but a small number of shares. The average sold by Merrill Lynch was only 9.7 shares per buyer.

Henry Ford and his son, Edsel, had originally put most of their stock into the Ford Foundation to keep from paying inheritance taxes after the senior Henry's death. Henry also was wise enough to make certain that the family held 40 percent of the voting stock, which they continue to hold today. This would keep Wall Street and takeover artists from running the company at any time in the future.

Safety

Safety became a greater concern within Ford as highway speeds increased and more cars were put on the road each year. The company had been working with the Cornell Medical College, the American College of Surgeons and the National Safety Council for two years to isolate the major causes of injuries in crashes. These were identified as doors springing open throwing people out of the car, people striking hard surfaces within the car and drivers being thrown against the steering column.

Ford started a program to build safety into its vehicles, promoting it as Lifeguard Design, which became the advertising theme for the year. With statistics stating that a person was twice as safe in an accident if he remained

within the car, Ford developed double-grip door latches, which were much more likely to keep the door closed during an impact. In earlier crash studies, doors sometimes flew open during a side impact. The safety door latches helped keep the doors closed

Timeline

- American television news program, *The Huntley-Brinkley Report*, debuts
- Grace Metalious's *Peyton Place* is published
- Famed NASCAR star Curtis Turner wins the Southern 500 in a '56 Ford
- Film actress Grace Kelly marries Prince Rainier III of Monaco
- Heavyweight boxing champion Rocky Marciano retires without being defeated
- Rock 'n' roll singer Elvis Presley records *Heartbreak Hotel*
- Ford Motor Company goes public with stock offer in January
- Interstate Highway construction begins what will ultimately become a 41,000-mile system
- Chrysler introduces push-button automatic transmission
- Ford now offers seat belts as an option
- Movie of the year: *Around the World in Eighty Days*

The Fairlane Victoria was the second most popular model in the Ford lineup, second only to the Fairlane Town Sedan. The Victoria had a much cleaner profile than the Crown Victoria body style, evidenced by its sales performance. (Photo: Ford Motor Company)

Three-across seating was standard in the 1956 models. The optional belts only came in pairs, protecting the driver and right-hand passenger. The deep-dish steering wheel was part of the Lifeguard safety package.

Dropping the rear armrest down in a Victoria gave it a sporty, four-seater feel.

Even with the spare tire, the trunk space was ample in a Ford. The patterned floor mat was standard.

The Thunderbird Special V-8 was added to the option list shortly after the new model introduction. This 312 cubic-inch engine put out 225 horsepower with a Fordomatic and 215 with a manual transmission.

The Lifeguard design, Ford's first effort at building a safety reputation, was incorporated into all its cars for 1956. This included a deep-dish steering wheel, optional lap belts and padded dash and padded sun visors. Ford also added what they termed "double grip" door latches to better withstand opening in an impact.

Crown Victoria models were more costly than the basic Victoria and carried an overload of chrome. Ford produced only 9,209 of the chrome "Crown" units compared to 177,735 Victorias.

This pre-production Customline was unique in that it was based on the Victoria body style. There was no B-pillar on this particular car (the dark vertical line is from the windows being rolled up on the far side of the vehicle) but it was never put into production with this trim combination. (Photo: Gary Richards collection)

during an accident, retaining the passengers within the cabin.

To lessen the possibility of passengers becoming injured inside the cabin, Ford added new "expanded" plastic dash padding to its option list and recessed the control knobs in the dash. Advertising literature claimed that Ford had dropped an egg on the padded dash from two stories up and it didn't break.

The steering wheel was changed to a "deep-dish" design with the center hub recessed three inches below the outer rim. This standard-equipment wheel contained no airbag, but would lessen the seriousness of chest injuries during a crash compared to earlier designs.

Of course, the most substantive improvement in safety that year was Ford's new seat belt option. The belts were made of aircraft-grade nylon-rayon cord and came with a simple, smooth-surfaced buckle latch that would help keep the occupants in place in a sudden stop or crash. They were rated to hold up to 4,000 pounds of force, a thousand pounds more than required by airline standards. Ford made the belts available across the entire model line, including the Thunderbird.

The company also sponsored a small safety conference and invited an Air Force colonel to speak on the advantages of restraints for occupants of vehicles in crashes.

In a test sometime earlier, the colonel had ridden in a test sled, crashing into a solid wall at 30 mph to show that with proper restraints, a driver or passenger could survive the G-forces of the impact.

This, combined with the studies, gave the Car Planning department direction and they began considering additional possible safety features for Ford's future.

The engineering staff had made enough progress for the company to announce that optional seat belts and a padded dash would be available for the 1956 models. Oddly enough, early advertising literature for Ford's new seat belt option featured 1955 model Fords, indicating that late '55 models may have been equipped with the belts.

Ford was given an award by *Motor Trend* magazine in 1956 for the most significant contribution to automotive progress. This year it was awarded in recognition of Ford's Lifeguard Design safety program.

Products

On September 23, 1955, dealers opened up showroom doors to a waiting public anxious to see the new '56 model Fords. Although body styles were very similar, there were some styling refinements and many hidden changes to make this particular model a much better car than Ford had ever produced in the past. Fords now had four series, 18 body styles and Y-block V-8 power available across the board. The Thunderbird for '56 started production on October 17, 1955, and was introduced to the public on November 2.

Body style changes to the full-size Fords were small and included rectangular parking lamps, a new hood ornament that sank into the hood, a new chrome strip across the rear deck and a large "V" chrome piece over the deck lid lock. The front grille was still concave, but had a different bar pattern in place of the '55 mesh grille. On the front fender was a new rocket-like V-8 emblem. A slightly different chrome side strip made its appearance on the Fairlane models. Also, the chrome trim around the 1955 model's headlamps was now gone in favor of body-color paint.

Kissin' cousin of the Thunderbird... '56 FORD

Another Ford marketing strategy was to show similarities between the Ford sedans and the Thunderbird. Ford positioned the Thunderbird as a flagship of style for the company and hoped to sell sedans by association.

New Models Added

Ford models now consisted of the Fairlane, Customline, Mainline and Station Wagon series. The Fairlane line included the new Fordor Victoria model with no B-pillar. It had a sporty look but still carried the practicality of a 4-door. The full-width rear doors went so deep into the rear of the car that the door handles were directly under the rear C-pillar. This gave rear passengers plenty of room for entry and exit. It also had the top-of-the-line side molding identifying it as a Fairlane. The molding had more flair and style than its lesser sibling, the Mainline model.

The standard Victoria 2-door model was still the sexiest-looking vehicle from Ford aside from the T-Bird. The Town Sedan and Club Sedan Fairlane models shared the same exterior trim, but carried conventional B-pillars.

Crown Victoria models were still identified by the chrome strip across the roof. The chrome strip was nonstructural and didn't have a pillar beneath the band.

This "Go Safer, Go Ford for '56" print ad strangely enough promoted protection against injuries and Thunderbird horsepower all on the same page.

Fairlane trim on the '56 could easily be spotted from the '55 by the single "spike" shooting down on the door. The three-spoke steering wheel was of the deep-dish safety design.

Ford dropped the transparent top speedometer for 1956 in favor of a more conventional dash layout. The backlit versions of 1954–55 were never well received. This Sunliner had a painted dash—with no optional safety pad.

Rear seating in the Sunliner was quite reasonable, seating three when necessary. The rear windows rolled all the way down and ash trays in the armrests were standard.

The Fairlane Sunliner played a part in stock-car racing along with the Victoria models. NASCAR sanctioned a convertible series for all the major tracks in the south and Fireball Roberts and Curtis Turner drove them successfully against the Chevys and Oldsmobiles.

Fifty-eight thousand Sunliners were produced in 1956, compared to almost 50,000 the year before. A new 12 volt electrical system was a major improvement for the '56 models and a good reason collectors today prefer them over the '55 cars.

Although the front end treatment didn't appear to change from the 1955 Thunderbird, the T-Bird emblem did change. The '55 used crossed checkered flags over the grille and the '56 models came with the turquoise 'Bird emblem.

The 1956 Thunderbird added wind wings as standard to help deflect some of the rushing air off of the occupants. Handling of the '56 was compromised primarily because it had the extra weight of the continental kit hanging off the rear.

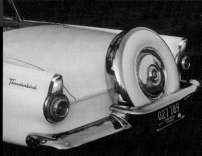

The dual exhausts now exited through the rear bumpers at the far edges. The year before, they exited through special chrome "bullets" mounted on the bumpers.

A major complaint on the '55 was a lack of luggage space. The continental kit helped solve that problem without redesigning the whole body and was a standard factory item for the Thunderbird this year.

The Thunderbird steering wheel was redesigned from a two-spoke to a three-spoke wheel. The speedometer stopped at 150 miles per hour, well past the actual top speed.

The '56 F-100 pickup is one of the most sought after by collectors today. The truck was probably one of Ford's all-time great designs. It came with a 12 volt electrical system and an overhead-valve V-8 that made it a real hot rod.

The Skyliner version of the Crown Victoria continued the 1954–55 traditions with a transparent Plexiglas half roof. The Plexiglas was great-looking but could contribute to a very warm interior during the summer months, and it scratched easily if not washed with a soft cloth and a mild soap. It came with a zip-up opaque ceiling liner to block out the sun when the heat and glare became too much.

Customline and Mainline

The second-tier Customline models came in either a Fordor or Tudor with chrome molding different from the Fairlanes. The entry-level Mainline series had no chrome side moldings and was somewhat stripped compared to the more costly models. According to the August, 1955, brochures, the I-6 engine was available in all

models except the Thunderbird, but the 272 cubic-inch V-8 with either 173 (manual) or 176 horsepower (automatic) were the choices in Customline and Mainline models. The Fairlane and Station Wagon models had a choice of the six-cylinder or the Thunderbird 202-horsepower 292-CID V-8. Later in the model year, all engines were available in all sedan models. T-Bird came only with either the 292 cubic-inch V-8 or the optional 312-CID Thunderbird Special. This hot powerplant sported 215 horsepower with a manual transmission or 225 with the Fordomatic.

Thunderbird

The 1956 Thunderbird was mildly freshened with the main exterior appointments being portholes in the roof pillars and a standard

The cab on an F-100 had a wraparound windshield. The rounded rear window was optional and came with chrome trim around the glass.

The '56 F-100 had a new grille and a new cab design. This would be the last of the smooth, rounded bodies on a Ford truck for many years.

continental kit at the rear to add badly needed luggage space. Wind-wings were also added to the doors at the front A-pillars, a mesh grille made its appearance and the dual exhausts were routed out cleanly through the rear bumper. The large rear bullet-style exhaust exits of the '55 were gone. The '56 exhaust setup looked great, but both versions were hard on the chrome plating after a few years of usage. Fresh air now came through a cowl-mounted vent.

The hardtop for the '56 models could be had with or without the portholes. During the

The graceful roof line of the Victoria was a carry over from 1955. A smaller chrome strip across the back of the deck lid and a large chrome "V" over the lock were new for '56.

1955 production run only tops without portholes were produced, but it soon became apparent this created a bad, possibly dangerous, blind spot. The porthole was added during early 1956 production to help the driver's rear three-quarter vision. The fiberglass top still came as standard equipment with a soft top as an option.

Thunderbird also featured standard Lifeguard door safety latches. A padded dash and sun visors were key safety options.

Station Wagons

The station wagons were grouped as one model lineup, but there were obvious giveaways that told the customer which model was the equivalent of each of the sedan models. For instance, it was clear that the Ranch Wagon was on par with the base Mainline sedans, the Custom Ranch Wagon and 6-passenger Country Sedan were equal to the Customline series sedans and the Parklane and oddly enough, the 8-passenger Country Sedan, were both trimmed with Fairlane moldings. The Country Squire with simulated wood paneling was on a top level of its own.

Trucks

Nineteen fifty-six was another big year for Ford pickups and trucks. Although the body styling was not unlike the 1953 to 1955 models, there were substantial changes including a completely new greenhouse with a wrap-around front windshield, and two choices for a rear window. The standard rear window was four feet wide and came with large pillars, but an optional wrap-around rear window gave far better visibility and came with chrome trim around all windows.

The interior dash layout was becoming more carlike than before and the top-of-the-line Custom Cab models had foam padding over springs for ultimate truck comfort in 3-across seating. The speedometer was a wide, easy-to-read instrument with temperature and fuel gauges below. It used warning lights for oil pressure and battery charging levels.

Power for the 1956 Standard and Custom Cab models included the renamed Cost Cutter six-cylinder producing 133 horsepower and a 272 cubic-inch overhead-valve V-8 with 167 horses. In a lightweight pickup,

1956 Model Car Pricing		
	Six-cylinder	V-8
Mainline		
Tudor Business		
Sedan	$1595	$1688
Tudor Sedan	$1690	$1783
Fordor Sedan	$1732	$1825
Customline		
Tudor Sedan	$1773	$1866
Fordor Sedan	$1816	$1909
Fairlane		
Fordor Victoria	$2061	$2154
Club Sedan	$1873	$1966
Town Sedan	$1916	$2009
Victoria	$2010	$2103
Crown Victoria	$2144	$2237
Crown Victoria		
Skyliner	$2208	$2301
Sunliner convertible	$2163	$2256
Station Wagon series		
Ranch Wagon	$2001	$2094
Custom Ranch		
Wagon	$2061	$2154
Country Sedan		
(6-passenger)	$2105	$2198
Country Sedan		
(8-passenger)	$2227	$2320
Parklane		
(6-passenger)	$2227	$2320
Country Squire	$2325	$2418
Thunderbird		
Convertible		$3151

All Fairlanes, Victorias and Sunliners came standard with four-ply, 7.10 x 15 tubeless tires. This model was equipped with Ford's I-REST tinted safety glass all around.

the optional V-8 created quite a hot rod. The F-100 pickup came in either a standard 110-inch wheelbase with a 6.5-foot bed or the optional 8-foot bed with a 118-inch wheelbase.

Engineering Changes

New Thunderbird V-8s

Ford's 223 cubic-inch inline six-cylinder this year had 137 horsepower when teamed with any of Ford's transmissions choices. It was an overhead-valve design featuring a cast block, 8.0:1 compression ratio, four main bearings and a one-barrel Holley carburetor. The base Y-block V-8 was a 2-barrel "Twin-Jet" version of Ford's 272 cubic-inch engine. It produced 176 horsepower with

Fordomatic or 173 horsepower with the manual or overdrive transmissions.

The Thunderbird V-8, 292 cubic inches with a 4-barrel carburetor, produced 202 horsepower with the Fordomatic transmission and 200 horsepower for cars equipped with the manual or overdrive transmissions. The 312 Thunderbird Special V-8 with a Holley 4-barrel (Double Twin-Jet) was the top engine option when the lineup was introduced in November, producing 215 horsepower with manual or overdrive and 225 horsepower with the Fordomatic. The five-main-bearing engine had an 8.0:1 compression ratio and came with an automatic choke and dual exhausts. All engines for '56 were rated for use with regular gas. Later in the production year,

a twin 4-barrel version of the 312 engine was put into limited production and was rated at 245 horsepower. The automatic choke, 4-barrel carburetor and anti-fouling sparkplugs were new for 1956. But one of the more notable improvements was the new 12-volt electrical system. This system provided much more electrical power to handle many of the new accessories and best of all, better starting power.

Racing

Ford was starting to provide more factory support for NASCAR stock car racing teams by 1956 and by mid-year started winning regularly. Out of 56 events that year, Ford won 14 and 13 of those were during the second half of the season.

One interesting letter to an owner from Ford, verifying the originality of a 312 cubic-inch engine with two 4-barrel carburetors, indicated there was a "homologation" production run late in 1955 to satisfy regulations for NASCAR racing.

Three racing superstars driving Fords that year were Glenn Fireball Roberts, Ralph Moody and Curtis Turner. Their major competition was coming from Chryslers, Dodges and Mercurys. Chevy only had four wins that year, but together with Ford, would dominate the 1957 season.

Mr. Donald Miller

Dear Mr. Miller:
With regard to your inquiry of July 1970, please be advised of the following:

Subject vehicle 1956 Ford Sunliner WGV105867 was produced in late 1955 and was equipped with a 312 cu. in. Ford Thunderbird Special engine.

The equipment you have described, Twin 4 bbl. Carburetors and dual point distributor were part of a 245-hp. engine option offered in model year 1956.

Several convertibles, 250 or more, were equipped with this engine (homologated) to allow them to compete in NASCAR Convertible events in the Southeastern United States (i.e., Daytona Beach, Fla., Darlington, S.C.).

The vehicle would also have a factory tonneau cover and boot kit with a B6A prefix.

It is impossible to verify the actual production number or dealer delivery location at this point: however, it is reasonable to assume this is one of those limited production models.

Sincerely,

Richard S. Levely
Industrial Relations

To fathers with children who drive

You may be the best driving teacher in the world. Your son or daughter may be as cautious as can be. But, it is only natural to worry when they are on their own in a car. For, as you know, there is much which experience, alone, can teach.

But learn to drive they *must*. So what can you do to help protect *your* offspring while they are gaining driving experience?

We at Ford think that Lifeguard design in the '56 Ford can go a long way towards easing your mind. You see, it gives the fellow at the wheel and all his passengers added protection should an accident occur.

Ford, working with universities, medical associations and safety experts found that

the majority of accident injuries were caused by the driver hitting the steering post, occupants being thrown against hard surfaces or from the car completely.

To give added protection against these hazards, Ford developed a Lifeguard steering wheel with a deep-center structure to act as a cushion in the event of accident . . . Lifeguard double-grip door locks to give extra protection from doors springing open under shock . . . shatter-resistant Lifeguard rearview mirror . . . optional Lifeguard cushioning for instrument panel and sun visors to lessen injuries from impact . . . optional Ford seat belts that keep occupants securely in their seats for greater safety. In short, Ford's Life-

guard family means that you and *your* family are safer in a '56 Ford.

There are many more things that make Ford a sound investment, such as, years ahead Thunderbird styling and the Thunderbird V-8 engine (the standard "8" for Fairlanes and Station Wagons and optional "8" for Customline and Mainline models). Visit your Ford Dealer and get all the facts on Ford and its Lifeguard Design.

'56 Ford
The fine car
at half the fine car price

"To fathers with children who drive" was one of many safety print ads Ford produced in its effort to promote the Lifeguard Design safety program for 1956.

▶

Ford's all-new Skyliner hardtop-convertible is shown here with the new world headquarters, only a year old, in the background. (Photo: Ford Motor Company)

FORD

The Year 1957

The '57 Thunderbird was an all-new body but destined for only a one-year production run. The sleek, slanted fins and longer overall body length gave this model what future collectors would be looking for.

Nineteen fifty-seven was an interesting year. General Motors' new-car share fell by almost six points, from 50.7 percent in 1956 to 44.8 percent in 1957. Ford was up almost two points, to 30.3 percent, and Chrysler gained three points for an 18.3 percent share of the market. Imports were starting to take off, more than doubling the 98,000 units sold in 1956. Germany, Britain, France and Sweden led the way in import sales. Japan was in eighth place in the import race for 1957.

For 1957, Ford introduced the Skyliner retractable hardtop, the supercharged 312 cubic-inch V-8 and the Ranchero car/truck hybrid. The company also regained the sales lead over Chevrolet for the first time since 1927.

The 1957 model cars were being built to a higher quality standard and had a clean, well-accepted body design. For the first time, Ford offered two separate wheelbases. The Fairlane and Fairlane 500 series sat on a 118-inch wheelbase and were a cool 207 inches long. The longer wheelbase gave these models a leg up in ride quality and interior roominess. Ford was proud of the size and advertised it as "a car so big, so daringly styled, you'll hardly believe it's in the low-priced field. Each model is over 17 feet long, and only a scant 4-2/3 feet high!" All other models were on a 116-inch wheelbase chassis.

Body styling for 1957 included a flat, low-contoured hood for better forward visibility. Hinged at the front, the new model's hood opened from the rear and was less likely to fly open on the highway. The '57 models were quieter than previous models due to the use of rubber-isolated body mounts.

Industry Trends

During the 1950s, 2-door sedans and 4-door sedans lost market share as the newer-style wagons and the stylish hardtop coupes made substantial gains. General Motors had a coupe in each of its lineups and Ford, a couple of years behind, made great inroads with the Victoria coupe after its introduction in 1951. By 1957, the industry sold more of the sporty hardtop coupes than any other model. The chart on page 127 shows how the models of all U.S. manufacturers sold between the years 1949 and 1957, giving a picture of how station wagons and hardtop coupes charged up the industry sales ladder.

For the buying public, 1957 was the year of the option. Talk of the customer wanting better mileage and economy of operation turned into more comfort options, automatic transmissions and V-8 engines to power them. Of the six million cars produced in the

U.S. during 1957, 82.5 percent of them had automatics installed. In high-priced vehicles such as Lincoln and Cadillac, automatics represented 100 percent of production. V-8 engines, introduced in almost all of the low- and medium-priced vehicles by 1955, now captured 83 percent of all car orders, bumping the six-cylinder back to 17 percent.

Convertibles made their best showing since 1949, finally climbing back up to 4.6 percent of the market. Some body styles, such as the business coupes with their deleted back seats and Spartan accouterments, were easy modifications. It wasn't a problem to justify keeping them in the lineup, even with their low sales figures. On the other hand, convertibles were a difficult engineering exercise and expensive to produce considering the small percentage of the market they enjoyed. But the open-air cars drew customers to showrooms and were viewed as flagships for the bigger companies, a must for the market.

Racing

Ford was deeply involved in stock-car racing by 1957, including the various forms of competition featured at the annual Daytona Beach trials. The cars competed on the famous beach for the flying-mile events where the driver got a running start and blasted through a one-mile trap to measure top speed. Daytona's four-mile beach/highway course was used for 160-mile-long convertible and hardtop races as well. Going head-to-head with Chevy for the manufacturer's championship, Ford hosted an all-star team of drivers that included Fireball Roberts, Paul Goldsmith, Marvin Panch and a winning guest appearance at a Bremerton, Washington, racetrack by Parnelli Jones. In '57, Ford won 26 of 53 events to Chevy's 21. Olds

and Pontiac were the only other winners, at four and two wins respectively. Ford was clearly the champ for the season.

Dean McCann was a two-year employee with Ford in '57 and drew the exciting assignment to support the Fords for the flying-mile beach event. "The first thing I noticed on the dual 4-barrel Fords was all this plumbing [extra gasoline lines]," said McCann. He walked up to Don Sullivan, father of Henry's flathead V-8 and now overseeing the racing program and said, "What is all that stuff? That isn't stock," and Sully said, "Shut up, kid." The extra fuel lines were installed by Sullivan to overcome a hot fuel-handling problem that could result in vapor lock. The outbound fuel line ran back to the gas tank and circulated constantly to keep it cool instead of boiling in the carburetor.

McCann and the team were working on a Thunderbird with a supercharged 342 cubic-inch V-8 driven by Danny Ames. The 430-horsepower T-Bird won the Champion Spark Plug Trophy for Fastest Time, covering the standing-start acceleration run at 97.9 mph. Thunderbird also won the two-way flying-mile event, with driver Ames topping 160 mph.

The Daytona Grand National races on the beach in the 1950s varied in length, depending on when high tide came in. These

contests ranged from 160 to 200 miles. There was one event for hardtops and another for convertibles.

Nineteen fifty-seven was also the year that the American manufacturers decided to withdraw from auto racing, specifically stock-car racing at such courses as Darlington and the beach course at Daytona. They even decided not to sponsor a pace car at Indianapolis for the Memorial Day 500-mile event. The cost of racing was now a whopping $7 million annually (the cost of one NASCAR racing team today is more than $10 million) and they were beginning to choke on the costs. The manufacturers were also starting to worry about the public connecting speed directly to a rise in highway fatalities and decided it would be better to get out of the business.

All three major manufacturers agreed to the longstanding

The Fairlane 500 model was another big stretch for Ford. For the first time, Ford offered two wheelbases in its sedan series. The 500 model sat on a 118-inch wheelbase and all other models were at 116 inches. (Photo: Ford Motor Company)

The Thunderbird frame cleared the ground by 5.3 inches and had a much larger luggage compartment for '57. Both the ride and handling of the new T-Bird was improved over the first two models.

Ford designers decided to overcome the problem of no trunk space and a heavy continental kit with one solution – a longer body with a larger trunk area. The '56 was actually longer, but only because of the "kit" hanging off the rear bumper. The new 'Bird could hold both luggage and a spare tire.

Interiors for the Thunderbird were luxurious with a padded wrap-around dash, deep-dish steering wheel, color-keyed fabrics and an instrument cluster that included a tachometer, speedometer and signal-seeking radio.

The elegance of the Thunderbird is what set it totally apart from the Corvette. Sales continued to climb as Ford prepared for next year's four-seater.

The 1957 model Thunderbird was 1/2 inch lower than the '56. Padded sun visors and dash were standard.

Four basic engines were available in Ford sedans, convertibles and wagons. The Thunderbird 312 Special V-8 and the Mileage Maker Six were for any model. The Thunderbird 292 V-8 was for the Fairlane, Fairlane 500 and Station Wagon models and the 272 V-8 was available only in the Custom and Custom 300 models.

Ford built 1,500 dual 4-barrel Thunderbird 312 V-8 engine Fords in 1957 to qualify its usage in NASCAR. Under the hood, the engine looked normal except for the dual bumps in the top of the air cleaner. Another special, low-production engine offered in all models for 1957 was a 300-horsepower supercharged 312 V-8.

Thunderbird had two engine choices for 1957—a 292 cubic inch 212 horsepower V-8 or the more powerful Thunderbird Special 312 cubic inch model that produced 245 horsepower.

requests of the American Automobile Association and the National Safety Council to slow down the horsepower race in their products. The companies were asked to withdraw from racing, decrease horsepower in all models and not promote performance and speed in their advertising. It was much too late to do anything about the horsepower race, because the 1958 models were almost ready for introduction, so the power increased an average of 20 percent in most models. Mercury was still the horsepower king, with a 400-horse engine and Lincoln-like horsepower available in all of its models. Rambler, on the other hand, would reduce engine power in 1958 to a mere 185 horsepower.

Ford Division stated that it would sell all of its racing cars, and the drivers would be cut loose by July 1. The companies didn't really throw it all out the window, though. The racing teams just became privatized—with quiet help from the companies. The manufacturers made a point of not advertising speed, but mentioning horsepower in a way that suggested that it helped in climbing hills, passing cars on highways or helping to operate the power options on the new vehicles. The average engine output in a standard sedan going into 1957 was 227 horsepower. This had been going up by about 30 horsepower per year.

Although advertising did take on a different look for a while, the hot engines were still there and so were Darlington and Daytona with all major models being represented. The racing teams had enough engines and parts to keep them in business. The famed Fireball Roberts won eight events single-handedly. By September of '57, Ford was at Bonneville setting 24-hour speed records and preparing advertising to show their "durability" by averaging 110 miles per hour for 24 hours

straight with another stock model recording a two-way salt flat run of more than 130 miles per hour. The ban did little to slow Ford down.

Products

The new Fords were low and sleek, with Thunderbird-style fins, standing at only four feet eight inches high—four inches lower from road to roof than the 1956 models. This was accomplished by dropping the seating area down between the frame rails that actually increased headroom four-tenths of an inch over the previous year.

The body design was another George Walker-team effort with Bill Boyer and Frank Hershey leading the actual design work. Walker joined the company as a vice president in 1955, and had given Ford its successes with the 1949, 1952, and 1955 series body styles as an independent industrial designer. Walker described the '57 body design as a new level of crispness. "The car definitely has a fleeter, lighter, faster line. See how the flair balances out both front and rear." Walker said he didn't like the word "fin." He thought they should be called instead "relief from severity or something." Walker wanted to lead the public toward cleaner designs. "Good, simple lines are the best expression of forward motion. With sculptured sheet metal, we can try to lead the public away from chrome."

Custom and Custom 300

The new Ford lower-line series on the shorter, 116-inch wheelbase provided the customer with the new body style of the '57 Ford but without the Fairlane price. The Custom series, replacing the Mainline and Customline series, offered engines from a six-cylinder to the Thunderbird V-8, was 16 feet long and carried a family of six without a problem.

Rear fin, bumper and taillight identification clearly separated the three classic years of Thunderbird. The '55 has vertical fins and large, bullet-like exhaust exits.

The '56 Thunderbird has vertical fins, exhausts exiting the bumpers and a continental kit.

The '57 Thunderbird has slanted fins, no continental kit and new design bumpers with exhaust exits.

The Business Sedan, a 2-door model with only a front seat and space in the rear for a salesman's cargo, was still available in the Custom line. Two- or 4-door sedans were available throughout the Custom and Custom 300 lineups. Ford still used the "Tudor" and "Fordor" spelling for these models.

The Custom 300 series, on the same wheelbase, had nicer side trim, a different two-tone paint scheme and nylon cloth interiors trimmed with vinyl. These also had a soft-tread floor covering and the full line of engine options.

Styling on the Ford had what one magazine described as "eyebrow headlights and flaring fins." The Fairlane script and a new hood ornament were mounted prominently on the hood and front body panel.

All of the new Fords had 14-inch wheels with fatter tires for better handling. With Ford's 312 cubic inch engine rated at 245 horsepower, acceleration from 0-60 miles per hour was 9.6 seconds.

This Custom 300 Fordor provided a classy look for those who couldn't afford to buy into the Fairlane series just yet. Ford built 194,877 of the clean looking Fordors. (Photo: Ford Motor Company)

New for 1957 was the Ford retractable Skyliner model. This replaced the glass-top Skyliner series of 1954–56. (Photo: Howard Voigt)

Fairlane and Fairlane 500

The Fairlane series was based on the longer 118-inch wheelbase, giving Ford the chance to provide their owners with a car to move up to without going to General Motors or Chrysler. The top-of-the-line Fairlane had more interior space than its sister models and extra trim inside and out. The interiors sported a handsome, new instrument panel with no knobs protruding past the surface of the dashboard for safety. Even though the safety theme of 1956 had not been a sales success, Ford stayed the course, feeling that this was an important issue to support.

The steering wheel was even more dished than in the past and had a smaller diameter for quicker steering.

Fairlane sedans had a thin new center pillar that was hidden by chrome window frames when the doors were closed. This gave the appearance of a Victoria "pillar-less" look. The B-pillar was 50 percent narrower from the top of the door to the roof, but full-sized behind the body and connected to the frame with four bolts.

Fairlane 500 Sunliner

The Sunliner convertible came with a weatherproof vinyl interior in a number of color combinations. Both Thunderbird Interceptor V-8 engines were available, as were all transmissions.

The Country Squire wagon still had the wood look, but was now a combination of decals and fiberglass trim. All wagons were on the 116-inch wheelbase. (Photo: Ford Motor Company)

Body Style Trends for U.S. Carmakers—1949 to 1957

Body style	1949	1950	1951	1952	1953	1954	1955	1956	1957
4-door sedan	49.2%	48.7%	50.8%	52.2%	50.3%	46.6%	38.4%	34.6%	31.9%
2-door sedan	42.8%	40.6%	33.2%	28.1%	28.1%	26.3%	21.1%	19.3%	14.6%
Business coupe	1.6%	1.3%	1.0%	0.6%	0.6%	0.3%	0.1%	0.1%	0.2%
Hardtop coupe	0.2%	4.0%	9.1%	12.4%	13.7%	17.1%	27.3%	31.2%	33.9%
Convertible	4.2%	3.1%	2.7%	2.3%	2.6%	2.8%	3.0%	3.4%	4.6%
Station wagon	1.7%	2.1%	2.8%	3.9%	4.8%	6.3%	9.6%	11.0%	14.6%

Source: *Automotive News*

The convertible weighed in at 3,637 pounds, nearly 460 less than the Skyliner retractable hardtop model that tipped the scales at 4,094 pounds—the heaviest of the Ford lineup.

Skyliner Retractable Hardtop

In the design works for several years, the Ford Fairlane retractable hardtop was a sensation for 1957. Introduced to the public on December 8, 1956, at the New York Auto Show, the uniqueness of the vehicle was a hit with the audience. They loved the idea, though not new, of a hardtop sliding all the way down into the trunk.

The fold-up hardtop had been originally designed for Bill Ford's Continental Mark II. A young engineer named Ben Smith was hired away from General Motor's Fisher Body to head up the project. According to Ben Smith's book, *Skyliner*, the Continental prototype retractable known as MP #5 was completed by January, 1955. The car was quite popular for internal management shows, but the decision was soon made to kill the Continental project and move ahead with the Ford. Ben Smith's team was actually contracted to work on the project for Ford as Continental employees. By August, 1955, the program received the final approval from top management.

Although the Skyliner project was running at a feverish pace to

"The Miracle Car of this generation," read the copy. Ford produced 20,766 Skyliners in its first year, about a third of the Sunliner production but respectable nonetheless.

The all-new Fairlane 500 was something Ford wanted to promote with its grace and style. Longer and lower than anything else in its class, the Ford was ready to take on Chevrolet for the sales lead after coming so close in 1955.

make the deadline for 1957 model production, Ben Smith and his team kept everything on schedule. In March of 1956, Smith was promoted to Advanced Lincoln engineering, but was required to keep an eye on the progress of the retractable to assure meeting the schedule. By late 1956, the new model was ready for production and news of the amazing new convertible was leaking out to the press.

The retractable was unique within the automotive market and appeared to be the answer to those wanting a convertible without the headaches of a rag top. The all-steel hardtop shielded passengers from inclement weather and folded neatly into the oversized trunk for summer fun. In reality, the hydraulic system controlling the folding top was complex and would occasionally stick in place halfway through the process, although the quality testing at

final assembly was thorough. The roof, with a 12-inch front-hinged flap, took up almost all of the storage in the trunk, leaving only a small, fenced-off center section for luggage. If the top got stuck, the driver could use a hand crank to raise or lower the top manually. The Skyliner had ten solenoids, seven high-torque motors and 610 feet of wiring to operate the all-metal roof structure. Although 20,766 Skyliners were sold in 1957, Ford had spent many millions developing the low-volume vehicle and never came close to recouping its investment.

The Skyliner was available with two Interceptor V-8 engines—the 332 Special V-8 or the 300-horsepower 352 Interceptor. Only Cruise-O-Matic was available with the 300-horse engine. The frame was a reinforced X-frame, similar to the Sunliner convertible.

Smith went on to design a

1966 Mustang with a manually operated hardtop convertible that never made it to production.

Station Wagons

Ford wagons for 1957 came in five models: a 2-door, 6-passenger Ranch Wagon; a 2-door, 4-passenger Del Rio Ranch Wagon; a 4-door, 6-passenger Country Sedan; a 4-door, 9-passenger Country Sedan; and a 4-door, 9-passenger Country Squire. All were available with either a Mileage Maker Six or any of the Thunderbird V-8 engines except the 272 version.

The new wagons had a new liftgate and tailgate structure. There was only one release and when the tailgate was opened, the catches that held the upper liftgate were released, allowing it to open automatically about one-third of the way. There was also additional cargo space in the 6-passenger

Thunderbird Optional Equipment

	Factory List Price	Dealer Retail Price
Fordomatic	$166.40	$179.80
Overdrive	100.70	108.40
Power Seat	59.30	63.80
Power Windows	93.80	101.00
Tinted Glass	30.00	32.30
Heater, fresh air	69.60	73.75
Heater, circulating	44.60	45.40
Power steering	63.80	68.70
Air conditioning	277.30	295.00
Selectaire with heater	395.10	412.50
Power brakes	34.40	37.10
312 cubic-inch engine	40.00	43.10
Radio, 6-tube	68.60	73.80
Radio, 8-tube	92.30	99.40

Dearborn delivery prices only. Delivery and shipping charges extra.

wagons with the rear cushion and seat folding flat to add easy-load space. The deck length in all wagons was now 106.5 inches, providing plenty of space to sleep in the wagon without opening the rear doors. The wagons were offered in eleven solid colors and twelve two-tone combinations.

Options for 1957

Some of the items on a growing and interesting option list were an Aquamatic windshield washer-wiper, deluxe rear antenna, exhaust deflectors, locking gas cap, outside rearview mirrors, portable spot and utility lamp, rear seat radio speaker and a tissue dispenser. One unique accessory was the auto-home electric shaver, the precursor to driving distractions such as today's cell phone. But the businessman always looked freshly shaven when arriving at work without so much as a razor nick.

Ford and its dealer network saw options as a way to improve the bottom line on cars. Many

of the options could be had from the factory, but the dealer could also add the same items after the sale. Factory-installed power brakes, seats, windows and steering were becoming increasingly popular by 1957.

Thunderbird

The '57 model, though certainly a sibling of the 1955–56 models, was definitely an all-new body but destined for only a one-year run. The sleek, slanted fins and longer overall body length gave this model what future collectors would be looking for. The continental kit was dumped in favor of more style. Overall length of the '57 was actually four inches shorter compared to the '56 with its rear-mounted tire, but the body of the new model was longer, which allowed for a larger, longer trunk area. This housed the spare tire and still had room left for golf clubs and a small suitcase.

For 1957, Thunderbird's adjustable steering column was still standard but the power brakes, steering and windows were options. The power brakes were so sensitive that, according to Ford, you could put a light bulb between your foot and the brake pedal and bring the car to a full stop without breaking the glass. The power steering cut effort by 75 percent.

The standard removable hardtop could be ordered with or without porthole windows and certainly provided the best winter environment for the driver. These were available in any body color for matching or two-tone effects. The optional soft-top was manually operated and folded out of sight behind the seat back with minimal trouble. Black, blue or tan versions were made of rayon and the white top was vinyl.

A new transistor-powered Volumatic Signal-Seek radio was now "instant on," unlike the previous vacuum-tube models,

1957 Model Car Pricing

	Six-cylinder	V-8
Custom		
Business Sedan	$1679	$1772
Tudor Sedan	$1783	$1876
Fordor Sedan	$1830	$1923
Custom 300		
Tudor Sedan	$1890	$1983
Fordor Sedan	$1937	$2030
Fairlane		
Club Sedan (2-door)	$2010	$2103
Town Sedan (4-door)	$2057	$2150
Club Victoria (2-door)	$2063	$2156
Town Victoria (4-door)	$2124	$2217
Fairlane 500		
Club Sedan (2-door)	$2053	$2146
Town Sedan (4-door)	$2100	$2193
Town Victoria (4-door)	$2167	$2260
Club Victoria (2-door)	$2106	$2199
Sunliner convertible	$2261	$2354
Skyliner (retractable roof)		$2942
Station Wagon series		
Ranch Wagon (2-door)	$2071	$2164
Del Rio Ranch Wagon (2-door)	$2161	$2254
Country Sedan Wagon (6-passenger)	$2211	$2304
Country Sedan Wagon (9-passenger)	$2309	$2402
Country Squire Wagon (9-passenger)	$2428	$2521
Ranchero series		
Ranchero	$1918	$2011
Ranchero Custom	$1966	$2059
Thunderbird		
Convertible		$3134
Hardtop		$3299

which needed warm-up time. It was unique in that it would raise the volume automatically as road speed increased. A rear-mounted antenna was available for the automatic-volume radio.

The power seat had a four-position memory. When you turned the ignition off, the seat would automatically move back for an easier exit, and when you started the engine, the seat

The sport look for a less expensive Ford came in the Custom 300 Fordor or Tudor. It had hub caps instead of wheel covers, a B-pillar body design but could be bought with any engine combination including the 245 horsepower 312 engine.

would return to one of four pre-selected positions to fit the driver's preferred setting.

There was a big jump in horsepower for the new 'Birds with both a 292 and 312 cubic-inch version available. The 292 cubic-inch V-8 with a 2-barrel carburetor produced 212 horsepower with a 9.1:1 compression ratio and was available only with the manual transmission. The 312 cubic-inch engine was initially available only with 245 horse-power, but later on, 270- and 285-horsepower versions teamed with an overdrive transmission or Fordomatic were added to the option list. The 245- and 270-horse versions both had 4-barrel carburetors, but different camshafts. The 285-horsepower engine was equipped with dual 4-barrel carburetors and all 312 engines came with a 9.7:1 compression ratio.

One low-volume engine for 1957 that saw its way into a few Thunderbirds was a 300-horse-power Paxton-McCulloch supercharged 312 screamer. These were homologated by

building 300 of the blown T-Birds for sale to the public. Many turned up at the Daytona NASCAR beach trials, such as the standing and flying-mile events. Twin exhausts were standard on all models. Larger drum brakes helped reduce brake fade under heavy use in the new Thunderbirds. The new 14-inch wheels dropped the over-all height and road clearance. The frame cleared the ground by 5.3 inches.

Ride and handling of the new T-Bird were improved over the first two models. With a trace of understeer, it slipped through tight corners without a problem in situations where the previous model would have had the rear end meeting the front. *Motor Trend* writers indicated that it was surefooted, had tight steering with 3.5 turns lock-to-lock and 0-60 mph acceleration of 9.5 seconds that would out-drag most cars. "The wheel falls nicely to hand and the steering lock coupled with better footing makes the new 'Bird handle very well, with but a trace of understeer."

Ranchero

The '57 Ranchero was a pickup based on a car body and chassis. Ford had actually been building this style of vehicle since the 1940s in Australia, where it was called a UTE, or utility vehicle.

The idea seemed to catch on for Ford and customers liked the idea of not giving up car comfort, accessories and handling to be able to carry cargo.

It came in either the standard Ranchero model or the Ranchero Custom. Both models were available with a 144-horsepower 233 cubic-inch six-cylinder, a 190-horsepower 272 cubic-inch V-8 or a 212-horse-power 292 cubic-inch V-8.

Sales of the Ranchero in its first year were very good. The standard model sold 6,418 units and the Custom stood at 15,277. With a total of 21,695 sold and very little additional investment required on Ford's part, the Ranchero was substantially more profitable than the 20,766-unit Skyliner.

Truck

Trucks for 1957 were substantially different from previous years. The new body design was very boxy, with a large, flat hood, a larger wraparound windshield and two distinctly different beds. The standard Flareside bed was similar to earlier years, coming in both 6.5- and 8-foot lengths. But the addition for 1957 was a no-cost optional Styleside box with smooth, slab sides and more carrying space.

1957 Ford Engines

	Displacement	Horsepower	Compression Ratio
Ford	223 (six)	144	9.1:1
Ford	272 (V-8)	190	8.6:1
Thunderbird *	292 (V-8)	212	9.1:1
Thunderbird Special	312 (V-8)	245	9.7:1
Thunderbird Super V-8**	312 (V-8)	270	9.7:1
Thunderbird Supercharged Special***	312 (V-8)	300	8.6:1

*212 horsepower with Fordomatic and 206 with manual transmission
**Two 4-barrel carburetors
***Paxton-McCulloch Supercharger

Engineering Changes

Chassis Redesign

The 1957-model Fords were another big step in changing the lineup over to a more solid, better handling group of sedans. Now featuring a "cradle-style" chassis, the frame bowed out under the floor pan, enabling the interior to sink lower, down in between the frame rails, bringing the seating arrangement down almost four inches lower than in earlier models. Even the convertible used the same frame with an additional X-style frame for support that kept the seats a little higher than in the sedans. The new models handled better and the new, smaller steering wheel gave it a feeling of quicker steering response. *Motor Trend* summed it up by saying, "Violent cornering brought out the advantages of a low center of gravity. This Ford really sticks." The writers felt that the body lean was modest and the good handling gave a feeling of confidence when driving hard through the corners. Ford's ride height was substantially lower than its 1957 Chevrolet competitor.

Suspension

Ford had pioneered the ball-joint front suspension in 1954, well ahead of most other manufacturers. For '57, engineers designed the lower A-arms to move both up and rearward under compression, softening the impact harshness of a pothole or bump. The rear leaf springs were elongated for a better ride and the overall handling was substantially better.

The 1957 Ford F-Series pickups were totally restyled, completely different from anything Ford had ever built. With Ford accounting for about two-thirds of the trucks on the road in 1956, they felt that this was the time to turn the heat up another notch on Chevrolet. (Photo: Ford Motor Company)

1957 was a year of new models for Ford. Not only was Thunderbird restyled, but on top of all new sedan styling and the new Skyliner, Ford introduced the Ranchero. This was in response to Chevrolet's Cameo truck line with the stylish fiberglass bed. The Ranchero was a combination car and truck and Ford produced 21,695 in its first year. (Photo: Ford Motor Company)

Interiors

Ford interiors had some changes this year, with fresh air brought in through a cowl vent just in front of the windshield, some 40 inches off the ground. This provided fresher air than scooping it in through the grille or side vents.

The dash of the new Fords was a one-piece unit, contoured to curve gracefully at the ends. The control knobs and the ashtray were recessed to keep the passengers from being impaled during an impact. The glove compartment door was designed to double as a cup tray when in the open position. Unlike the cup holders of today, it was not meant to hold drinks while the car was in motion.

The industry was finally making gains through research with the major suppliers in producing more durable enamels that were both chip- and fade-resistant. Until now, most buyers were skeptical of buying a red or brightly colored car because it would fade rapidly after a few months in the sun. Ford used a new enamel formula for its '57 models that was much more fade-resistant. In tests in the Florida sun, where ultraviolet rays and rain had caused serious weathering and fading on earlier models, the new paint tested three times more resistant than the 1956 paint samples.

The Dana Corporation developed the Powr-Lok limited-slip differential for the 1956 Packard, sending power directly to the rear wheel with the most traction. By 1957, it was available in Chevrolet, Pontiac, Oldsmobile, Rambler, Studebaker, Packard and Lincoln vehicles. Borg-Warner's version of limited slip was available later in the year, designed for most of the remaining vehicles, including Fords.

More Engine Choices

Ford engines were still producing plenty of horsepower across the board—especially in the low-priced range. Thunderbirds could be had with either the 292 or 312 V-8 engines. For other models, there was the Mileage Maker six-cylinder, Ford's overhead-valve engine producing 144 horsepower. The Custom and Custom 300 series vehicles had two engine options: the 272 V-8 at 190 horsepower or a jump to the 312 V-8 with 245 horsepower. The Fairlane, Fairlane 500 and wagons all came with either a six-cylinder, a 212-horse, 292 cubic-inch V-8 or an optional 312 Thunderbird Special V-8 with 245 horsepower. Ford had also developed a special, late-addition, 312 cubic-inch Super V-8 producing 265 horsepower. Ford literature described this as, "... a regular production option available only to selected customers who qualify for competition power!"

For the first time, Ford introduced machined, wedge-type combustion chambers that replaced the normal cast surfaces. This made for more efficient combustion and superior mixing of the fuel and air charge for more economy and power. The intake manifolds on the V-8s were larger, the valves were also larger with greater lift and there was a new camshaft. Standard dual exhaust went away in '57 except on the 245-horsepower 312 cubic-inch engine option. The 223 six was standard on the Custom and the 272 V-8 was the base engine for the Custom 300. On the Fairlane the six was standard and on the Fairlane 500 and most station wagons the 292 V-8 was the base powerplant while the lower-line wagons also had the six.

▶

The Thunderbird for 1958 was a new car with seating for four. It sold almost 39,000 units in its first model year despite an abbreviated nine-month run. (Photo: Ford Motor Company)

FORD

The 1958 Thunderbird now seated four. The new styling included a fully functional hood scoop, a mesh screen grille and dual headlamps surrounded by wing-like front fenders.

The Year 1958

With an economic recession in place through much of 1958, the car-buying public was tightening its belt, waiting to see how the economy shaped up before looking too seriously at the new models. For the first time, America seemed to be losing some of its love of big cars as sales for smaller ones climbed at a steady rate. The sales performance of imported cars made unprecedented gains along with much healthier sales for the small, new American Motors Rambler and Studebaker Lark. Journalists were predicting that small cars would soon take over the market and the big car would be doomed. But apparently the recession had as much to do with sales of the less expensive small vehicles as did their popularity.

By the fourth quarter, both Ford and Chrysler were back in the black after losing money for the first three quarters of the year. Ford lost more than $28 million in the third quarter alone but GM and American Motors were in the black for the entire year, putting

Top Imports for 1958

1	Volkswagen	78,225
2	Renault	48,050
3	English Ford	33,425
4	Fiat	21,175
5	Hillman	18,900

a stop to Ford Division's one-year sales lead over Chevrolet.

By April, 1958, Senator A.S. Monroney's new price-disclosure bill started to gain strength. Until then, the manufacturer's suggested retail price on a car was held closely by the dealer and rarely disclosed to a buyer. The prices for one model could vary greatly from state to state or even city to city. The public wanted some kind of a standardized price from the manufacturer that would be uniform throughout the United States. The bill finally received support from the manufacturers, dealers and the public and was voted into law in May. The first Monroney window sticker would be on 1959 models in the fall of 1958.

Products

Dual headlamps, new body styles and a 4-seater Thunderbird marked the 1958 model year for Ford. This new headlamp configuration provided an advance in illumination. With dual headlamps, the second, dedicated high-beam lens was designed to focus much farther

down the road. The older system used one lens per side and simply provided more light on "bright." The dual headlamps also gave the manufacturers a chance to sell a totally new look to the customers and were standard on all models, including the new 4-seat Thunderbird.

The suspension layout was basically the same as in 1957, but air suspension was an extra-cost option on all Fairlane and station wagon models. With the option, air-filled bags substituted for coils at the front and trailing arms and a lateral track bar were used at the rear. This was the only year Ford offered the air-suspension option, because it really provided no advantages over coils, wasn't as reliable and was far more costly to produce. Ford wasn't ready to take a loss on it, customers weren't ready to pay extra for it and by the introduction of the 1959 models, the option was gone. Chevrolet, Oldsmobile and Pontiac chose to continue offering the air suspension for their full lines in '59.

There were two new engines this year. A 332 cubic-inch V-8 was standard on the Fairlane, Fairlane

500 and wagons with a 300-hp 352 Interceptor V-8 optional. The 332 V-8 was offered as an option on the lower-line Custom and Custom 300 models and the 352 engine was standard on the Thunderbird.

Ford sedan models were again based on two different wheelbases—116 and 118 inches—and body styling was substantially revised from the previous year.

The all-new 4-seat Thunderbird now came on a 113-inch wheelbase and became the first Ford to feature unit body construction.

Custom 300

The lower-line Ford sedans had less trim inside and out, but a great number of the options were shared with the Fairlane series. All engines except the 300-horsepower Thunderbird engine were available. Two-tone exterior color combinations were optional as well, but in different schemes because the Custom 300 used different side trim treatments than the Fairlane and Fairlane 500 models. It came with a single driver's-side sun visor and armrest, a chrome horn button in the center of the steering wheel (no horn ring) and chrome window moldings.

Fairlane and Fairlane 500

The Fairlane was the least expensive model on the longer 118-inch wheelbase. It came with a large, half-oval-shaped chrome side strip to differentiate it from the Fairlane 500 series. The 500s had longer, narrower chrome trim, with a wide, gold-colored section on the rear fender.

The sportier Fairlane 500 series represented the top-of-the-line Fords. It included Fairlane trim and came with a standard 332 cubic-inch V-8. Or you could get the optional, new 352-CID powerplant for stronger

acceleration, horsepower and torque. Both engines came with the Cruise-O-Matic transmission, a high-performance automatic designed for better economy on the highway and excellent off-the-line response in town.

The power steering on the '58 was light but still had plenty of road feel, considering comparable units during this period. With 4 1/2 turns lock-to-lock, the steering was fairly slow compared to the Plymouth Fury at 3 1/2, but the Chevy Impala took five turns. The Fairlane, with a 352 V-8 and 4-barrel carburetor, put out 300 horsepower and was quite agile in traffic—both in handling and power.

There was more noticeable front-end dive under hard braking than on the 1957 models, suggesting that lower-rate front springs were chosen in favor of a softer ride instead of better handling. This also allowed excessive body roll in the corners.

Ranchero

The Ranchero "car-truck" was now in its second year, available in either standard Ranchero or Ranchero Custom trim. The upper-level Custom added items such as foam-rubber seat cushions, armrests on both doors,

a sun visor for the passenger, a horn ring and a cigar lighter. It also had extra chrome trim on the exterior and 11 two-tone color schemes. Both base and Custom levels offered three engine choices: the 144-horsepower Mileage Maker six-cylinder, 205-horsepower 292 V-8 and 300-horsepower 352 Interceptor Special—the same as the Thunderbird. The manual or Fordomatic transmission could be teamed with any engine and Cruise-O-Matic could be had with the Interceptor Special V-8.

Options such as four-way power seat, power windows, power brakes and power steering gave the Ranchero all the comforts of a car, but it still had a bed to haul lumber.

The Fairlane Sunliner was one of Ford's top-of-the-line models. Not only was it sporty looking but in the manufacturers' horsepower race, Ford made an Interceptor 352 Special V-8 with 300 horsepower available as an option on all Fairlane, Fairlane 500 and Station Wagon models. (Photo: Ford Motor Company)

The "coffee table console" ran the length of the interior and housed a radio speaker, power window and heater controls and ash trays. Window controls were located within reach of any passenger.

Optimum illumination was provided with the new headlamp layout by using the outside lamps for the low beams and a combination of both for high beams.

The rear seats didn't pretend to house more than two passengers. The center console ran from the dash to the rear seat.

The unitized construction had a major advantage over the body-on-frame in getting rid of the squeaks and rattles. The entire body was dipped in rust proofing prior to assembly.

Trunk space in the earlier "classic" 'Birds never looked so good. The new Thunderbird had 20 square feet of luggage space plus a full size spare tire. Ford claimed room for four suitcases, two golf bags and extra gear.

The Thunderbird was available with 12 solid colors and 17 two-tone combinations. The body featured unitized construction for the first time and provided advantages in interior seating and a lower silhouette for exterior styling.

Styling for the half-ton-capacity Ranchero featured a 1958 front end, but still used the 1957 rear end with single circular tail lamps and fins. Rancheros became popular with contractors who wanted some style on the work site, but still needed the practicality of a truck, even though it was a lightweight compared to regular pickups.

Station Wagon

Station wagon models, ranging from the base Ranch Wagon to the top-of-the-line Country Squire, shared a wide range of engine options with the Fairlanes. It didn't matter if you wanted the lowly 145-horsepower Mileage Maker Six or the 300-horsepower Thunderbird Interceptor Special V-8, you could get it. The wagons also had a full array of options, such as fender skirts, backup lights, Polaraire Conditioner, signal-seeking radio, spotlight with mirror and bumper-mounted exhaust deflectors. The Ford-Aire Suspension was also optional on wagons equipped with a V-8 engine and automatic transmission. These molded nylon-rubber air-filled cushions replaced the coil springs at all four

Sales Positions: 1957 vs. 1958			
1957 Position/Sales	Make		1958 Position/Sales
2.... 1,456,288	Chevrolet	1	...1,233,477
1.... 1,493,617	Ford	2	...1,028,160
3....... 595,503	Plymouth	3	390,774
5....... 371,596	Oldsmobile	4	306,473
4....... 394,553	Buick	5	263,871
6....... 319,719	Pontiac	6	229,707
12......... 91,469	Rambler	7	186,180
7....... 260,573	Mercury	8	136,121
8....... 257,488	Dodge	9	135,481
9....... 141,209	Cadillac	10	122,545

corners and had the advantage of load leveling, maintaining even ride height at all times. But they weren't as reliable as steel springs and sometimes lost pressure.

Thunderbird

The new Thunderbird model for 1958 was completely redesigned to accommodate four passengers. The marketing staff knew that although the 2-seater model was a great-looking flagship for Ford, a 4-passenger model would have a much larger potential market,

and design work was started in earnest in late 1955. Ford Motor Company sold more than 1.6 million vehicles in 1957 and Thunderbird accounted for only 21,380 units. This was far greater sales than the 'Vette had achieved, but not large numbers for Ford. Ford Division head Robert McNamara was a finance man, not into wasting money or manpower. McNamara saw the potential gains of upsizing the 'Bird. The new model, even though it was introduced only in January of 1958, managed to find its way to

The most fascinating part of a Skyliner is watching the intricate maneuvers taking the roof into the trunk. The front 12 inches of the hard top folded up to make the package fit into the trunk.

Cruising down the road in a Skyliner was as good as being in a Sunliner, but when the winter season set in, the hardtop sealed out the weather and noise while keeping the heat in. The Sunliners weren't totally weather tight.

almost 39,000 buyers in its first model year—less than a nine-month run!

A program to create a new Thunderbird with more passenger and luggage room had been underway for three years. It was first planned to be built on a stretched 1957 'Bird chassis, but this wasn't working out well. The engineers then saw plans for a Lincoln unit-construction body and decided quickly that this might well be the answer for their new, larger Thunderbird challenge. Their primary goals were to seat four passengers in complete comfort, provide a low car with easy entry and exit, an interior that would be safer than any other car and an engine that would pin the driver to the back of the seat. The first prototype was completed in April of 1957 with the new roofline and general overall new dimensions, but with a '56 T-Bird rear end and front fenders.

Walker and Associates was dedicated to designing home appliances from the early 1930s to the mid-'40s. George Walker considered the woman's point of view in appliances and carried this theme, long before it was popular, over to automotive design. You can see some of this thinking in the 1958 Thunderbird's convenience features, ease of use, high fashion and softer design cues. George Walker gives credit for the design of the new 4-passenger Thunderbird to one of his chief stylists, Joe Oros, who later designed the original Mustang.

The hardtop version was introduced in mid-January 1958 and the convertible followed in May. With the fall introduction of the new sedans, Ford print advertising included the classic '57 Thunderbird because that was all that was available until the 4-seater introduction in January. In a May 1 press release

announcing the new Thunderbird convertible, Ford showed its red, white and blue colors.

Ford timed the introduction of its newest product to coincide with the annual worldwide May Day observance of the Soviets. Ford officials said the Thunderbird convertible is a dramatic contrast between the standard of living in the United States achieved under a free enterprise system and living standards in the U.S.S.R.

By the May introduction, the hardtop already had a backlog of more than 10,000 orders, keeping workers on heavy overtime schedules.

The new design included a unique hideaway system for the soft top. The rear-hinged trunk lid opened in reverse fashion and the top was lowered completely into the trunk instead of behind the seat as for earlier models. This took up more trunk space, but eliminated the usual convertible

The rear of the Skyliner was mammoth with a wider and longer rear section to house the hard-top and all the mechanical and hydraulic paraphernalia.

The front 12 inches of the roof had to fold completely under to fit in the allotted truck space. One of the weak points of the retractable program was a lack of training at the dealer level. Although the vehicles left the factory thoroughly tested, the dealers were not committed to preparing for continuing service.

All 1958 Ford sedans, trucks and Thunderbirds came with the new dual headlamps which greatly improved night driving.

The standard engine for 1958 Skyliners was now an Interceptor 332 Special V-8 with the new 352 Special as an option. Any transmission was available including Fordomatic, Overdrive, manual 3-speed and Cruise-O-Matic.

A special bin had to be cordoned off to contain the luggage because the hardtop and hardware had to be stowed around it, using much of the space.

Fairlane Skyliner interiors were upholstered with Royal Scot Tweed in a linen pattern with vinyl trim. The Selectaire conditioning was mounted under the dash from the factory. Dealers could also add the units to cars not so equipped.

The wide, boxy rear end on the Skyliner was different sheet metal than on other Fords and was a costly addition that Ford never recouped in sales. Only 14,713 Skyliners were produced that year, about the same as the Country Squire station wagon.

boot, which could be difficult to deal with and didn't have the clean, stowed look of the 1958 'Bird. This also left a full-width back seat with the top completely concealed inside the trunk.

The Thunderbird model line received the 1958 *Motor Trend* Car of the Year Award for the U.S. manufacturer making the most significant engineering advancements. This one was for building a car that combined safety with performance and comfort with compactness. Former Indy 500 winner Sam Hanks wrote in the *Motor Trend* article, "Ford has really looked into the safety situation. They've been working on it for a long time now, and it's my feeling that they've pioneered a lot in the field of interior safety, particularly. It's lucky that they were able to coordinate the wants of the stylists with the needs of the safety engineers." Many of the

safety items were improved carry over features from 1956 and '57, including the padded dash, concave steering wheel, sunken knobs on the dash and padded visors. The front seat backs were also padded on the 'Bird. There still was no locking mechanism to keep the seat back from folding forward in a sudden stop should a rear passenger come flying forward. Seat belts had yet to become standard equipment.

The 17-foot-long Thunderbird convertible was only 52.5 inches high, had a wheelbase of 113 inches (its sedan cousins were on 116- and 118-inch wheelbases) and weighed in at 3,733 pounds. This length might seem excessive now, but bear in mind that the Chrysler 300D was more than 18 feet long! The wheelbase for the 1957 Thunderbird was only 102 inches and total length was 15 feet, a full two feet shorter than the new 'Bird. The new model in

convertible form would weigh almost 800 pounds more than its smaller predecessor.

The only engine available in the Thunderbird this year was a 352 cubic-inch V-8 producing 300 horsepower at 4,600 rpm. Compression was 10.2:1 and the torque rating was 395 foot-pounds at 2,800 rpm. Hydraulic lifters and dual exhaust were standard and cold air was pulled in through the hood scoop to the 4-barrel carburetor.

Performance figures were interesting for the Thunderbird, with 0-60-mph times for the 300-horse engine at 10.1 seconds. Weighing in at 3,708 pounds, 400 more than the 1957 model, it took the extra 55 horsepower to move the new 'Bird hardtop off the line respectably. The convertible, introduced in June of 1958, weighed in with an extra 25 pounds over the hardtop. A prototype 375-horse version tested by *Motor Trend* magazine dropped the time to 8.1 seconds, but it would never see production.

Transmission choices were now extended to the standard manual 3-speed on-the-column (with or without Overdrive), Fordomatic and the new Cruise-O-Matic high-performance automatic. The Cruise-O-Matic could be started in the D2 position for a second-gear start on slick surfaces, or in D1 for normal driving. All models had a column shifter. Overdrive was optional on both automatics.

The interior console ran from the dash to the rear seats and housed many of the controls, including the heater, air conditioning, power windows and the radio speaker. This provided easy access for the driver and passengers. Seating was of the classic 2+2 arrangement. The '58 T-Bird had bucket seats for the first time and only the driver's seat was adjustable. The standard front passenger seat lacked fore/aft adjustment but an adjustable seat was an option. Rounding out the interior were a pair of rear buckets.

Ford began using Teflon-coated ball joints in the front suspension of the '58 Thunderbird for reduced wear and maintenance. Along with new outboard-mounted shocks and redesigned upper and lower control arms, the new 'Bird offered a firmer, better ride. It had 33 percent fewer parts than the previous year. Ford threw away the rear leaf suspension of the classic 1955–57 T-Birds in favor of a new coil-spring setup. Trailing arms with upper torque arms kept "wheel hop" to a minimum under hard acceleration and a track bar provided lateral stability. An air suspension was available to replace the coils at all four corners.

Assembly was a two-stage program with the unitized, spot-welded bodies being assembled by the Budd Company in Philadelphia. They were then shipped for assembly to the Wixom Assembly Plant, home of the Lincolns, located northwest of Detroit. There they were dipped in a rustproofing bath before moving to paint and then assembly. Thunderbirds ran down the same assembly line as Lincolns except for the interior installation.

Optional accessories for 1958 included backup lights, an electric clock, front fender ornaments, outside mirrors, radio, tinted glass and windshield with sun shade band, Magic Air heater, seat belts, Fashion-Ray wheel covers, whitewall tires and a high-pressure windshield washer.

Police Cars

In 1958, Ford sold more police cars than all other manufacturers combined. The company made all the right options available in an effort to attract this business. Custom 300 and station wagon models were the basis of a full array of optional suspensions, engines and specialty accessories.

A full lineup of engines was offered for serving everything from meter readers needing a Mileage Maker Six to the 300-horsepower Interceptor V-8 used by the Highway Patrol. Ford would ship from the factory with a red dome light, spotlight mirror, power brakes, power steering, exhaust deflectors, backup lights, rear antenna and a non-glare mirror. Heavy-duty front and rear seats were also an option, because many of these vehicles would be used 24 hours a day under heavy service.

Engineering Changes

Engines

Engine choices for 1958 sedans included a 145-horsepower Mileage Maker inline six, a 205-horsepower 292 cubic-inch V-8, a 240-horsepower 332 cubic-inch Interceptor V-8, a 265-horsepower Interceptor 332 Special and a 300-horsepower 352 cubic-inch Interceptor Special V-8. The Interceptor 352 was standard in the Thunderbird and optional in the Fairlane and wagon models and came with a choice of Cruise-O-Matic, Fordomatic, Overdrive or a manual transmission. Cruise-O-Matic was available only with the optional 265- and 300-horsepower Interceptor engines.

The 2-barrel version of the Interceptor 332 delivered 240 horsepower, ample torque and reasonable fuel mileage on regular gas. The 4-barrel version added another 25 horses and a difference you could feel. Combustion chambers were now being machined instead of just a cast surface, providing even mixing of fuel and air for better combustion.

The Ranchero was in its second year of production and Ford managed to push only 9,950 out the door, a drop of almost 12,000 units. (Photo: Ford Motor Company)

1958 Model Car Pricing

	Six-cylinder	V-8
Custom 300		
Business Sedan	$1799	$1923
Tudor Sedan	$1880	$2004
Fordor Sedan	$1930	$2054
Fairlane		
Club Sedan (2-door)	$2031	$2147
Town Sedan (4-door)	$2081	$2197
Club Victoria (2-door)	$2155	$2271
Town Victoria (4-door)	$2216	$2332
Fairlane 500		
Club Sedan (2-door)	$2173	$2289
Town Sedan (4-door)	$2223	$2339
Town Victoria (4-door)	$2289	$2405
Club Victoria (2-door)	$2229	$2345
Sunliner convertible	$2430	$2546
Skyliner (retractable roof)		$2907
Station Wagon series		
Ranch Wagon (2-door)	$2193	$2293
Fordor Ranch Wagon	$2243	$2343
Del Rio Ranch Wagon (2-door)	$2292	$2392
Country Sedan (6-passenger)	$2342	$2442
Country Sedan (9-passenger)	$2442	$2542
Country Squire (9-passenger)	$2563	$2663
Country Sedan Delivery	$1888	$1909
Ranchero series		
Ranchero	$1985	$2086
Ranchero Custom	$2046	$2147
Thunderbird		
Hardtop (soft top optional)		$3330

The top-of-the-line Interceptor, the 300-horse 352 V-8, wasn't going to help gas mileage any, but at 27 cents per gallon, that wasn't a big concern. This option also came with a 10.2:1 compression ratio. With larger ports and more direct runners, the intake manifold supplied on all the Interceptors was now designed to efficiently direct the fuel/air mixture into each cylinder. The engine's cooling system was under 13 pounds of pressure and with a pressure-sensitive radiator cap, there was no loss of coolant unless excessive temperatures and overheating occured.

Cruise-O-Matic

Most magazine car testing produced positive comments from drivers on the new Cruise-O-Matic transmission—especially when compared to the older-design Fordomatic. The Cruise-O-Matic gave plenty of control over which gears the driver could start out or stay in while accelerating or slowing down. Using D1 would always start the car in first gear and let it shift to second, keeping it there until the driver upshifted to third, but selecting D2 forced a second-gear start for better traction on wet or icy surfaces. The Cruise-O-Matic was also built with higher torque capacity to handle the larger engines Ford was now producing. A full-throttle start from D1 or Low would provide plenty of smoking rubber in almost any situation. Of course, tire smoke wasn't the only indicator of performance, as the big 300-horse Fairlane took a full 10.2 seconds to reach 60 mph from rest, according to *Motor Trend*. This was substantially slower than the comparably priced 305-horsepower Plymouth Fury that could go from zero to 60 mph in 7.7 seconds. The flip side, however, was fuel economy. While the 305-horse Plymouth got a highway average of 10.6 miles per gallon, the Ford jumped to 13.4 mpg. A 280-horsepower Chevy managed 14.6 miles per gallon in the same test.

Around the World

In 1957, Marty Ramashoff, a young movie producer living in Connecticut, went to Ford Division's advertising agency, J. Walter Thompson, with an idea for a 1958 Ford ad campaign. The 1956 movie of the year, *Around the World in Eighty Days,* had captured the public's imagination, and Ramashoff wanted to latch onto the theme for a series of Ford ads. "I went to them and said, 'Why don't you drive the new '58 Ford around the world in eighty days?' It turned out that it couldn't be done in eighty days, so the campaign became 'the first car ever to use the whole world as a test track.' It was amazing. We ended up making something like 30 commercials from the trip."

Ford felt that the public was weary of racing tests for advertising and that's when Ramashoff's idea came into play. He assembled a team consisting of hundreds of people. They started traveling, negotiating with far-off customs offices and consulates, attending foreign customs lectures and planning for all the thousands of details that would ultimately help the new Fords travel around the world.

The caravan consisted of two new blue-and-white Ford Fairlane 500 Town Sedans, a 1957 Ranch Wagon and two Ford F-350 trucks. The F-350s were 4-wheel-drive models loaded with water tanks, refrigeration units, supplies and spare parts to keep the crew of 18 clothed and fed for 2-1/2 months. The Ranch Wagon was designed specifically for the camera operators to follow in. Ford wanted the whole trip thoroughly recorded for history.

In the entourage of 18 were five experienced test drivers and a doctor. The rest had various skills at diplomacy, cooking and international finance and were generally culturally experienced. A total of 16 inoculations were required before the trip.

Socony Mobil (later Mobil Oil) arranged for the worldwide oil drops necessary to complete the trip. The Fords were tuned to operate on a standard grade of American fuel, but this wasn't available in many parts of the world they would be traveling.

The caravan left Detroit early on a July morning for New York, where it would board the *S. S. New York*, bound for London. The ship hit a whale during the crossing that apparently lodged itself on the bow, slowing the liner's speed and causing a late arrival. The team spent three days in London before flying with the vehicles to France. The team drove from Paris to Geneva and to Rome, then on to Venice, where the crew took a two-day break to rest while the cars were thoroughly prepared for the tough road ahead. They left Venice on August 5, 1957, for Trieste, Dubrovnik, Athens and Istanbul.

After directing one of the commercials in temperatures hitting 107 degrees in Greece, Ramashoff flew on to Bangkok and Japan. The Japanese government wouldn't let any American vehicles in the country in 1957. Even with Ramashoff and the J. Walter Thompson crew trying to negotiate for Ford in Tokyo, the cars were not allowed to enter—not even to shoot a commercial.

The going was getting very rough as they made it to Tehran and the real test started as they crossed the Khyber Pass. "Going through the Khyber Pass," recalled Ramashoff, "the cars took a tremendous beating but they both made it." Some of the countries, as today, had more than their share of dangers and conflicts, often causing a change in the planned route. "In Calcutta, we had a problem because there was some kind of a war going on in East Pakistan and later on encountered a civil war near the Malay Peninsula."

One of the surprises came in Yugoslavia on a crushed-rock road leading up a mountain range. Coming around a hairpin curve, one of the Fairlanes struck a large rock that hit the rear engine mount and moved the engine 1-½ inches out of line. The

Here's the '58 Ford in Turkey, on its way around the world. Thousands of rugged miles like this proved the performance of its new Interceptor V-8 engine.

Nothing newer in the world of power

Precision Fuel Induction a '58 Ford exclusive gives more power on less gas in new Interceptor V8 Engines

PROVED AND APPROVED AROUND THE WORLD

58 FORD

The Ford "Proved and Approved Around the World" campaign supported a trip around the world in two new 1958 Fords. The campaign was developed by Marty Ramashoff, a young producer living in Connecticut, who pitched it to Ford's agency of record, J. Walter Thompson. After weeks of preparation and a 110 day driving adventure, Ford launched a huge advertising campaign about the journey.

car continued running great, so they chose not to mess with a good thing—or as stock-car legend Junior Johnson said, "If it ain't broke, don't fix it." It finished the trip without a repair.

Also in Yugoslavia, a third of the crew came down with stomach troubles, which didn't help speed up the trip. In Turkey, the group drove through blinding sandstorms and camped in the desert with armed Turkish guards patrolling the campsite all night. Turkey was also the place where

one of the Fords hit an open 3-foot irrigation ditch at 40 miles per hour, but nothing serious broke and they moved on. Through Pakistan the daily average speed was almost never above 15 miles per hour. One of the crew said, "I was absolutely astonished by the durability of these '58 Fords. I had no idea they could be driven so hard by slam-bang professional drivers, week after week, over such horrible terrain, without breaking up." Other than major bangs and dents, the Fords apparently had

Ford pickups were not substantially changed for 1958, but quad headlamps were added in similar fashion to the cars. (Photo: Ford Motor Company)

daring motion picture project." The Filmways company produced the feature, which followed the Ford through England, France, Switzerland, Italy, Yugoslavia, Greece, Turkey, Iran, Afghanistan, Pakistan, India, Burma, Malaya, Thailand, Cambodia, South Vietnam and the United States.

The trip took 110 days to complete. Ford used television commercials and print ads throughout the year to promote the durability of the new models.

no mechanical failures and only regular maintenance during the trip. The only irregular option on the two Fairlanes was the "export springs," a heavy-duty option for some export countries that helped support the heavy loads being carried during the trip.

The automatic-equipped Fords ran well but all vehicles had to travel by rail car on four flatcars from the Thailand border to Bangkok because there were no roads through the dense jungles there. In Cambodia, they slithered through a muddy, almost impenetrable jungle and monsoon rains.

The program was expensive for its day, with costs for the advertising production pushing over $1 million and funding for the cars, parts and designated fuel stops well above that figure. "When you got past Greece and into Turkey, there was only Russian fuel which was very low octane," said Ramashoff. "So we had fuel dumps located at intervals with armed guards. There was a great photo of a large fuel barrel and a whole supply of parts with some guy sitting there with a rifle and Mt. Everest in the background." The high-octane fuel and parts supplies

were critical items they didn't want to lose.

Travel was also difficult for the crew flying ahead to meet the drivers. "Remember, I was living in Connecticut, and it took four days in a Boeing Stratocruiser to get to Bangkok," said Ramashoff. "We had a cameraman, an operator and an assistant, two electricians, two grips and a prop. It was as thin a crew as we could get and we traveled light. It was an amazing adventure."

"World" was the theme of each of the ads, including "Top brand in the wagon world," "Around the world in a brand-new fashion," and "Nothing newer in the world of power." These included photos of the 1958 Ford in Afghanistan, Greece, Turkey, Bangkok, Paris and San Francisco. In one photo layout featuring two new Fords and the Eiffel Tower in the background, the lead line said, "The Ford spoke French— and the French spoke Ford." It was "proved and approved around the world."

One interesting promotional strategy for the world theme was a film titled *One Road*. It was billed as "Around the World in a '58 Ford—American industry's most

The New York taxi fleet was often dominated by Checkers, but Fords competed well on initial buying price and long-term operating costs. This gave Ford a distinct advantage over most of its competition. (Photo: Ford Motor Company)

FORD

The Year 1959

In less than a minute the "world's only true hardtop convertible" could be hidden in the trunk for summer fun. This would be the final year for the slow-selling Skyliner.

Cars from Europe and even Japan were starting to show their strength, and the U.S. imported more than 600,000 cars in 1959. The smaller cars were popular and less expensive than the longer, lower, wider vehicles from Detroit. Buyers even purchased 480,000 new Studebaker Larks with their chopped-off front and rear ends. It wasn't the end of the big cars, not by a long shot, but small cars would now find their place in the profit structure of the Big Three. Chevy Corvair, Plymouth Valiant, Mercury Comet and Ford's Falcon would be introduced by the end of the year. And the Pontiac Tempest, Oldsmobile F-85, Buick Skylark and Dodge Lancer would follow them to market a year later.

The economy was taking a much better turn in '59 over the previous year, and Ford nearly caught Chevy in sales once more, losing by a mere 11,000 vehicles in the model year and actually beating GM in the calendar year. Unfortunately for Ford, the model year was what mattered.

Ford sheet metal underwent big changes once again, with George Walker saying this was the best design of his career—a stretch in anyone's book. The 1958–60 period of American car design was less than classic, but the Ford design was acceptable considering what other manufacturers were offering.

This year, Ford would drop its base Customline series, leaving the Custom 300 series as entry-level models. Later in the model year Ford introduced the new Galaxie with a unique-to-Ford sport roof.

Transcontinental Race Reenactment

Ford had been busy since Henry I started the company in 1903 and in 1959, it produced its 50 millionth vehicle at the Rouge Assembly complex. On June 1, Ford sent this new Galaxie vehicle off on a cross-country reenactment of the 1909 Great Trans-Continental Race: New York to Seattle. The event wasn't about speed but focused on getting good press coverage for the milestone vehicle. The white Galaxie 4-door sedan stopped at each city on the schedule, along with a new Ford truck, two more sedans, a Model T similar to the 1909 race-winning vehicle and a 1906 Model K. The Levacar show vehicle also traveled with the tour in an exhibit van. The Galaxie was shipped by air from Seattle to the World's Fair in Moscow after completing the cross-country tour in a well-orchestrated public-relations campaign.

Racing

Ford was still heavily involved in NASCAR racing, even after the temporary layoff in '57. The Thunderbird, which had never carried a Ford oval or crest, was not considered a Ford in the eyes of the popular sanctioning body and was listed separately in the records from full-size Fords.

In the inaugural Daytona 500 in '59, the just-opened 2-½ mile high-bank race was the setting of the closest finish in NASCAR history. Crossing the line after 500 miles of manhandling heavy Detroit iron, it was a photo finish, with the Thunderbird of Johnny Beauchamp and the Olds of Lee Petty. The 'Bird was declared the winner, but after studying the finish line photo for three days, officials decided it was the Olds of Petty that had won a place in history. Petty had slipped by the Beauchamp Thunderbird a mere 24 inches ahead. Detroit had proven that the big iron was durable on a super speedway, as the winning car ran the 500-mile event averaging 135 miles per hour—some 25 miles per hour faster than the Southern 500 at Darlington that year.

Products

Models for 1959 included the Custom 300, Fairlane, Fairlane 500 and the new Galaxie, announced to the public in December, 1958, and placed in dealerships by January. The exciting Galaxie included two

sedans, two hardtops, the Sunliner convertible and the last Skyliner retractable hardtop. There was also a full line of wagons including two Ranch Wagons, three Country Sedans and the Country Squire with its simulated woodgrain sides. The little-changed Thunderbird hardtop and convertible added only a new grille and minor trim modifications. The Ford air suspension option was dropped for 1959 due to lack of interest and high production costs.

The 1959 Fords featured new bodywork and other changes and were advertised as "the world's most beautifully proportioned cars." The body had been designed with a narrow rear, or C-pillar, but late in the process a design study with a much thicker pillar was shown to Ford executives. They felt the design was pleasing, but decidedly more costly and complicated to build. One of the problems was that the Ford steel mill at the Rouge couldn't produce a wide enough piece of steel to allow the roof and wider pillar to be stamped as a single piece. Finally it was decided that the new roofline could be important

enough to potential sales that the new pillars would just be welded onto the roof panel. This added a significant cost increase in production, because both metal work to dress the welded seam and a trim piece to cover the weld had to be added. Cost-conscious Robert McNamara was skeptical but finally agreed to use the Thunderbird-style pillar on the

Timeline

- Jack Lemmon, Tony Curtis and Marilyn Monroe star in film, *Some Like it Hot*
- Rock 'n' roll star Buddy Holly is killed in a plane crash
- Thunderbird finishes second in the inaugural Daytona 500—losing its place in history to Lee Petty's Olds by 24 inches
- Rod Serling hosts the *Twilight Zone* television series
- Sir Christopher Cockerell tests the first air-cushion vehicle
- Boeing 707 jet airliner enters service
- First flight is made by the X-15 rocket-powered research aircraft
- Alaska and Hawaii are admitted to the Union
- Ford produces its 50 millionth vehicle, a '59 white Galaxie, on April 29
- Robert Stack stars in film, *The Untouchables*
- Edsel ceases production of the 1960 model after a run of only 2,846 vehicles
- Movie of the year: *Ben Hur*

The Fairlane 500 Sunliner had some carry-over similarities to the 1957 and '58 models, but Ford was making an attempt to keep each new model year totally different than the year before. Seat belts were still an extra cost option. (Photo: Ford Motor Company)

Skyliner models were heavy and boxy looking, but the hydraulically operated fabric roof gave true convenience to summer and winter driving.

The Galaxie Sunliner trimmed with stainless-steel fender skirts and two-tone paint was an impressive sight. Painted skirts were also available.

In '59, the new Galaxie had a "floating star" style grille. This at first appeared to be an impossible task, but three suppliers quickly found a way to do it and it was put into production.

Trunk space was greatly increased with the large, squared-off rear-end design. It wasn't particularly appealing but it was practical.

After the body design on the 1959 model was signed off and approved, many within the company were still unhappy with the look of the grille, a horizontal-bar layout similar to window blinds.

The Ford team came up with a new "floating star" design but the engineers thought it would be almost impossible to produce.

Several suppliers were shown the design and asked to create a plan for production and a cost estimate. Three suppliers bid on producing the new star grille and had samples to show Ford within six weeks. After one company was chosen by purchasing, the new aluminum grilles were rolled out for shipment to the assembly plants without a problem.

Custom 300

The Custom 300 series, now bottom of the line, still included the Tudor, Fordor and Business Sedans. There was less and less call for this model, but it was so inexpensive to keep in the lineup that even in low volume it still made money for the company. Tudor and Fordor models usually came with either the 145-horsepower Mileage Maker six-cylinder or the 292 cubic-inch V-8, though the 225- and 300- horsepower Thunderbird Special engines were optional.

Fairlane and Fairlane 500

Fairlane models came in either a Club Sedan 2-door or a Town Sedan 4-door. These were much less sexy-looking than the Fairlane 500 series models that included the Club Victoria, Club Sedan, Town Victoria and Town Sedan. The Club versions had no B-pillar, which for the 1950s defined the sports coupe look.

new Galaxie models only and go with the thinner pillar on all other models to avoid the extra costs. Working out the production details and melding it in with the standard assembly line meant the Galaxie was to be introduced later than the other models.

Motor Trend magazine praised the interiors of the new Ford, its editors saying that finish and detailing of the Ford was better than its Plymouth and Chevrolet counterparts. The doors closed soundly, and the fit and finish of the body parts were very good.

By 1959, Ford was at the height of its "chrome" period, adding massive bumpers, grille and moldings to add extra sparkle all around the car.

The Custom 300 Business Coupe was $1,934 with a six-cylinder engine, the least expensive in the Ford lineup. All Business Coupes were for three passengers, reserving the space behind the front seat for storage only. (Photo: Ford Motor Company)

This Galaxie 500 was on display at the Brussels World's Fair. (Photo: Ford Motor Company)

When the Fairlane 500 name was first introduced, it was one of the first vehicle names associating a Ford with an auto racing heritage, a famous 500-mile event. In fact, the models actually used in stock-car racing were the lower-line Custom 300 vehicles.

Galaxie

This was the first year for the new Galaxie lineup, now the flagship of full-size Fords. This line had different chrome on the rear deck and body sides as well as unique interior dash trim and upholstery materials. Flooring was deep-pile carpeting, the door trim was special and cushioned armrests were standard. Galaxies also were the home of Ford's last Skyliner retractable hardtop, Sunliner convertible and pillarless 2- and 4-door sedans. Doors on all 1959 Fords were long, opening wide for easy entry and exit. But they could be difficult on paint in parking lots and other tight spots. The Galaxie was considered a separate line in the Ford family, but oddly enough, the rear deck

of all Galaxie models featured a Fairlane 500 badge just above the chrome "V" across the rear of the car.

Thunderbird

The Thunderbird received only minor exterior and interior changes for 1959, but the big news was the new 350-horsepower 430 cubic-inch V-8 derived from the Lincoln lineup. As long as fuel mileage wasn't an issue, the driver could tap into plenty of torque and acceleration.

The grille was now a horizontal-bar format instead of the original mesh screen in the '58 model. Minor trim on the side was also changed, moving to a chrome arrow look instead of the vertical hash marks. Wheel covers were changed slightly, but still looked bland. The 1958 'Bird had "Thunderbird" script on the front fenders but this was dropped for 1959. The T-Bird emblem on the rear pillar was changed to new bird wings forming a "V" look. This was added just before production started and was not

always shown in early publicity photography. Ford produced 67,456 T-Birds in 1959, almost twice the 37,892 made in 1958 and far beyond the 21,380 of the 2-seat 1957 model.

Because Ford dropped the air suspension option throughout the lineup, the T-Bird needed a new rear suspension for '59. It ended up with a much simplified leaf spring system that worked well and would have cost a lot less if Ford had used it in the first rendition of the new model, known as the "Squarebird."

Station Wagon

Seven inches longer than their '58 counterparts, the '59 wagons provided 17 percent more inside cargo space. Built on a 118-inch wheelbase, the Ford Country Squire and Country Sedan models could hold nine passengers, all facing forward. All power options available on the sedans, such as power windows, seats, steering and brakes, were available on the wagons as well. Other options were a signal-seeking radio, MagicAire heater, SelectAire Conditioner, visor-spotlight, nonglare rearview mirror and an electric clock.

The Country Squire model still had the imitation woodgrain siding. The Country Sedan was the only 2-door model left in the lineup. Any engine was available in any wagon.

Trucks

Ford introduced its first factory 4-wheel-drive option for the F-100 and F-250 models to compete with Chevy's version that had come out two years earlier. Engine options were the same as 1958 and the new 2-speed version of the Fordomatic was used as an option in the F-100 series. The body style remained the same but a new bar-type grille replaced the mesh grille of the previous model.

Engineering Changes

New Fordomatic

Fordomatic, Ford's automatic transmission since 1951, now became a 2-speed instead of a 3-speed. With no mid-range gear to downshift to, climbing steep grades was harder on the engine and acceleration times off the line were slower. But Ford weighed the lower manufacturing costs, simplicity and light weight of the 2-speed transmission against the higher warranty cost of a more complicated one and decided that performance-oriented customers would simply opt for the Cruise-O-Matic. Everyone else would

likely be satisfied with the 2-speed automatic.

Ford described the new aluminum-case 2-speed as less complicated, claiming 105 (27 percent) fewer parts, and as 22 percent lighter than the previous iron-case Fordomatic. Under heavy acceleration, the 2-speed Fordomatic would shift into high gear at around 58 miles per hour or under an easy foot, at about 18 mph. Fordomatic was available with any engine up to the 300-horsepower Thunderbird Special.

The more expensive 3-speed Cruise-O-Matic transmission was now offered as the "high performance" choice and was

available on any of the V-8 engines and standard in the 350-horsepower Thunderbird.

Engines

Engine options included the 145-horsepower Mileage Maker, a 223 cubic-inch inline six that ran on regular fuel, came with a manual choke and was available on all models except the Skyliner hardtop convertible. Three Thunderbird V-8s were available for the sedan lineup this year. The standard version on all models was a 292 cubic-inch, 200-horsepower V-8 with a 2-barrel carburetor and 8.8:1 compression, designed to run on

George Walker poses here with a new Thunderbird and a Model T. The T-Bird was highly successful in its second year of being a four-seater and quality was generally good. A close look at the photo, however, shows a problem with body fit between the hood and nose of the car. (Photo: Ford Motor Company)

turn the quarter mile in 17.5 seconds at 80 mph on regular fuel but would have been much happier on premium.

According to *Motor Trend*, fuel mileage for the 300-horsepower 352 V-8 engine was 17.7 miles per gallon at a steady 50 miles per hour, but stop-and-go city driving dropped it to 13.7 mpg. Meanwhile, cruising at 50 mph, a 305-horse Plymouth averaged 12.5 mpg, while the 280-horse, tri-power Chevy averaged 15 mpg.

If you were in the market for a new Thunderbird, Ford stretched one more time and offered a 430 cubic-inch Thunderbird Special with 350 horsepower (borrowed from Lincoln), the largest in the industry. All the V-8 engines came with an automatic choke.

The 1959 Ford lineup including the Thunderbird was honored with the Gold Medal of the Comite Francais de l'Elegance *for fashion at the Brussels World's Fair. William Clay Ford was on hand to accept the award. (Photo: Ford Motor Company)*

regular fuel. The 332 Special V-8 with 225 horsepower had an 8.9:1 compression ratio and a 2-barrel carb. The top-of-the-line power for Ford sedans was the 352

Thunderbird Special engine, with 300 horsepower. It came with a 4-barrel carburetor and 9.6:1 compression ratio. According to *Motor Trend* magazine, it could

Front Suspension

Engineers redesigned the Ford front suspension for easier and less expensive front-end alignments. They used slotted holes and serrated washers for adjustment to keep the front end in alignment for longer periods of time. Chevrolet was still using the

The "Thunderbird"-inspired roofline of this '59 Galaxie 500 4-door pillarless hardtop is clearly in evidence. (Photo: Ford Motor Company)

slot-and-shim method, which needed more frequent realignment, giving Ford a "lower maintenance" brag point. Steering was converted to a recirculating-ball system that minimized lost linkage motion and gave a positive feel. Earlier Fords sometimes had a "wandering" feel to the steering while driving down the road.

Ford's ladder frame provided much of the body stiffness and it was somewhat heavier for 1959 than it had been on the 1958 models. In 1957, Ford had bowed out the frame to bring the seating arrangement much lower to the ground and provide an overall height reduction of about four inches. For 1959, Ford took this even more to heart by moving the frame rails almost to the outer width of the tires. It wasn't lower, but the arrangement did make for more usable space in the interior. The tradeoff was a frame that needed extra stiffening at the rear, adding more weight to an already heavy vehicle. This caused excessive body roll in the corners, more than Chevrolet and Plymouth allowed in comparable models. Although the straight-line ride was smooth, the handling characteristics were anything but desirable.

Ranchero was now in its third year. With the optional 300-horsepower 352 V-8 it was a real hot rod. (Photos: Ford Motor Company)

Brakes

Brakes for the lineup came in three different sizes. The sedans had 180.2 square inches of brake surface, station wagons and the retractable hardtop had 191.4 and the Thunderbird brakes were the biggest at 225.5 square inches. The wagons, which were about 100 pounds heavier than the Thunderbird (not including any extra load they were likely to carry), probably could have used the 'Bird's brakes. Stopping power was adequate, but nothing to brag about. Fading could start to occur after about four or five hard stops in brake testing. Chevy was using grooved linings to help dissipate the heat and had fewer fade problems with its brakes.

The Country Squire still had that "woody" look about it, but any real wood was long since gone. The top-of-the-line Country Squire came standard with whitewall tires, full wheel covers and nine-passenger seating. (Photo: Ford Motor Company)

1959 Model Car Pricing

	Six-cylinder	V-8
Custom 300		
Business Sedan	$1934	$2044
Tudor Sedan	$2015	$2125
Fordor Sedan	$2065	$2175
Fairlane		
Club Sedan (2-door)	$2143	$2253
Town Sedan (4-door)	$2193	$2303
Fairlane 500		
Club Sedan (2-door)	$2255	$2365
Town Sedan (4-door)	$2305	$2415
Club Victoria (2-door)	$2311	$2421
Town Victoria (4-door)	$2371	$2481
Galaxie		
Club Sedan	$2303	$2413
Town Sedan	$2353	$2463
Club Victoria	$2359	$2469
Town Victoria	$2419	$2529
Sunliner	$2591	$2701
Skyliner		$3063
Station Wagon series		
Ranch Wagon (2-door)	$2339	$2449
Fordor Ranch Wagon	$2401	$2511
Country Sedan (6-passenger)	$2504	$2614
Country Sedan (9-passenger)	$2582	$2692
Fordor Country Sedan	$2745	$2863
Country Squire (9-passenger)	$2702	$2812
Country Sedan Delivery	$1888	$1909
Ranchero series		
Ranchero Custom	$2177	$2227
Thunderbird		
Convertible		$3368
Hardtop		$3631

New Enamel Paint

Making its debut this model year was a new kind of enamel paint, dubbed Diamond Lustre Finish. Ford literature claimed, ". . . you won't have to wax it . . . ever!" One brochure described the laboratory torture testing as exposing the paint to searing tropical sunlight and corrosive salt air for months. Then Ford engineers supposedly went after the new paint finish with BB guns to simulate stones and gravel a driver would encounter on the highway. "And again, Diamond Lustre proved its toughness . . . proved it's far more chip-resistant than Ford's famous enamels of the past!"

Gas Turbine Engine

Ford engineers developed a supercharged gas turbine engine in 1959 for possible use in a host of vehicles including passenger cars. The 300-horsepower engine, the 704, was small and light enough at 650 pounds to fit under the hood of a new sedan, required no warm-up period and would run on various fuels, ranging from jet aviation fuel to a light-grade diesel. Comparable diesel engines weighed around 2,700 pounds. Unlike previous gas turbine engines that employed only one stage of air compression, the 704 utilized two—the second being a supercharged stage.

Consideration was given for possible use as a generator, to power military tanks, heavy-duty tractors or even small locomotives. The low-speed compressor would turn at 46,500 rpm with the high-speed one screaming at 91,500 rpm. The exhaust gases exited the vehicle at 740F / 394C, about the same as a conventional car.

The 704 was first shown to the Department of Defense on Monday, April 6, 1959. Although Ford did some testing of the engine in vehicles, the powerplant proved impractical and costly to build and was soon moth-balled in favor of conventional gasoline engines.

Design Chief George Walker poses with the 1960-X dream car clay model. (Photo: Ford Motor Company)

FORD

Dream Cars of the Nineteen Fifties

1950 Muroc (Photo: Henry Ford Museum and Ford Motor Company)

Inexorably tied to the American Dream and the role personal transportation would play in the euphoric post–World War II era, the car was fast changing the ways Americans lived, played and went about their business. In the 1950s, Ford and other manufacturers learned the value of creating dream cars that were meant to spur the public's imagination. Ford showed these far-reaching designs at public events to build excitement and to monitor opinions on the likes and dislikes of the buying public.

1950 Muroc

The Muroc was a quarter-scale model from 1950 that featured high-rise fenders well before the early Corvette Stingrays. The headlamps were incorporated into the grille on either side of heavy chrome vertical slats. It had a hood scoop mounted on the center of the hood and a racy-looking 2-seat interior.

1952 Continental Nineteen Fifty X

This novel model was one of the better-looking concept cars built by Ford during the 1950s. It had practical styling and many of its design features were adopted in Lincoln and Mercury models a few years later. It incorporated automatic jacks for changing tires and a telephone and Dictaphone in the interior. It also featured automatic hood and trunk controls.

The engine was considered secret but incorporated "Turbo-dyne" high-compression combustion chambers and a "Multi-plex throat" carburetor and manifold system. Apparently only Ford knew what these terms meant, but they sounded very futuristic to an eager public.

The curved windshield blended into the clear dome top. The top would retract for good-weather driving into the leather-covered rear portion for a "Targa" effect. The concept stood 56.7

inches road to roof and total length was 220 inches, or 18.3 feet. It was sometimes referred to as the Nineteen Fifty X or the Continental X.

The "Car of Tomorrow" was first viewed in January, 1952, by 15,000 employees at a Ford Engineering open house in Dearborn. It remained a popular draw for crowds on the auto-show circuit and has an appealing design to this day, something that can't be said of too many of the dream-car designs of the 1950s.

1953 Syrtis

The Syrtis, a 3/8th-scale dream model, featured Ford's "Roof-O-Matic," the forerunner of the 1957–59 Ford Skyliner hardtop convertible.

A June, 1953, *Motor Trend* magazine article said, "The mechanism was designed with the thought of application to any of the company's passenger lines. Because such devices almost invariably debut as extra-cost items at the luxury car level, it seems safe to venture that Lincoln, Mercury and Ford will ultimately offer it in that order."

The top design was unique in that the rear window could be separated from the top at any time. It could be lowered into the trunk, allowing a "flow through" open rear window with the roof in place, left in place while the top was lowered into the trunk or moved forward just behind the driver's seat for a "tonneau windshield" effect. Typically, both would be stowed in the trunk space for a convertible conversion.

The interior featured a steering wheel with only a single spoke at the bottom of the turning arc. This was great for viewing the gauges, but a little weak in an impact. This hardtop convertible was never offered in a Mercury or Lincoln.

1953 X-100

The X-100 was a mildly freshened version of the Continental Nineteen Fifty-X. The former was

sent to Paris in September, 1953, for a four-day display at the Champs-Elysees Salon of Ford of France, then on to the Paris and London auto shows.

Crafted of steel and aluminum, this fully operational vehicle was a 2-door convertible 5-seater weighing in at a hefty 5,900 pounds. The eight miles of wiring in its 12-volt electrical system alone weighed 665 pounds. It featured a sliding half-roof that could be operated by a switch on the instrument panel or by added pressure on the door button.

A 300-horsepower V-8 with a newly designed manifold and carburetor powered the X-100. The electric adjustable front seats were equipped with seat belts.

Other interior accessories included an electric shaver, a 7-tube radio, Dictaphone and a telephone. It also had two horns: A loud one for country driving and a softer one for the city. This car design incorporated more than 300 pieces of aluminum, reducing weight by 250 pounds.

1953 Lincoln XL-500

The dream-car body of the XL-500 was laid over a 1953 Lincoln chassis with a "hot rod Lincoln" engine. With a graceful profile, tinted heat-resistant glass roof and a red and white leather interior, the XL looked like something that could become reality. The fiberglass body was painted scarlet red and measured less than 57 inches high. The bottom section of the body was formed of fiberglass and according to Ford, "Chrome is not used at all as pure applied decoration." This statement would have been hard to back up after viewing production Fords of the late 1950s.

This show vehicle, introduced at the March 14, 1953, Chicago Auto Show, was equipped with a telephone located on the console. Picking up the handset would automatically cause the horizontal antenna (protruding from the top of the windshield) to rise to a vertical position. It had controls on the console for a tape recorder

1952 Continental Nineteen Fifty X (Photo: Henry Ford Museum and Ford Motor Company)

1953 Lincoln XL-500 (Photo: Henry Ford Museum and Ford Motor Company)

and release buttons for the hood and trunk. Push buttons in the center of the steering wheel controlled the automatic transmission and a floor pedal operated the horn. Warning lights were located along the windshield header bar and the primary gauges and speedometer were housed in the top center of the dash, obviously for looks—not for easy viewing. Heat to the rear seat was transferred through the center console. "Reliable information" in a 1953 *Motor Trend* article announced that this car "may" feature the front end and the rear fender treatment of the 1954 Lincoln.

1954 FX-Atmos

"Automobile design ideas of the future, so advanced that up to now they have been seen only in Ford styling studios, were unveiled Friday, March 12 by Ford Division in a dream car, the FX-Atmos," said a March, 1954 *Ford News* article. "FX" stood for Future Experimental and "Atmos,"

according to Ford, denoted free and unlimited creative thinking. "It is not proposed as a future production vehicle, and for that reason, no engineering considerations have been involved in its development," said Ford Division general manager L. D. Crusoe. "But some of its features are within reasonable reach in terms of today's technology." The 220 inch-long car was displayed for the public March 13 to 21, 1954, at the Chicago Auto Show.

1954 XM-800

Out of the Mercury design stable came the Mercury Monterey XM-800 concept car. Described by Lincoln-Mercury general manager Benson Ford as "startlingly new but readily producible," the car easily could have gone into volume production. The 4-passenger hardtop was neither a sports car nor a dream car. According to Ford, it combined the best of both. The low-profile car, only 55.6 inches high, featured a concave grille, a wraparound windshield

and integrated bumpers. It was first shown at the Detroit Auto Show on February 20, 1954.

The interior featured individually contoured seats, a 4-way power seat for the driver, power steering and brakes, a tachometer and a Merc-O-Matic transmission. Ground clearance was a mere seven inches.

1955 Futura

The Futura, one of Ford's better known show cars of all time, was built in the Ford Styling Center under the direction of designer Roy A. Brown, Jr. in 1954 at a cost of $250,000. Brown later was picked as the lead designer for the ill-fated Edsel. The Futura was powered by a race-tuned, 500-horsepower Lincoln engine. It made its public debut at the hands of Benson Ford, cruising to Central Park for a press conference at the Tavern on the Green. The public relations staff put the Futura in front of the restaurant alongside a carriage and horse from Central Park for a photo

1954 FX-Atmos (Photo: Henry Ford Museum and Ford Motor Company)

1954 XM-800 (Photo: Henry Ford Museum and Ford Motor Company)

opportunity. When Benson fired up the Futura's hot V-8, the horse reared up and almost came down on the show car's fender. "It would have screwed up the whole program," said Ford public relations man John Cameron. "It kind of shook up everybody including Benson Ford."

The pearlescent Futura was 19 feet long, seven feet wide and 52.8 inches high. It had a heavy influence on the design of the 1957 Lincoln. After usefulness on the show circuit waned, the Futura was shipped to Metro Goldwyn Mayer Studios in Los Angeles and appeared in the film *It Started with a Kiss*, starring Glenn Ford and Debbie Reynolds. The car was purchased by Hollywood car customizer George Barris, who left the beautiful vehicle sitting out in the California sun at a gas station in North Hollywood for almost nine years. One day Barris got a call from a movie producer wanting a car—quickly—for a new television production of *Batman* starring Adam West.

1955 Futura (Photo: Henry Ford Museum and Ford Motor Company)

1955 Futura (Photo: Henry Ford Museum and Ford Motor Company)

1955 Mystere (Photo: Henry Ford Museum and Ford Motor Company)

Barris and his team had to turn the show car into a Batmobile in three weeks with a black fuzzy finish, fully radiused wheelwells and a completely changed hood and nosepiece. In an era when most experimental cars are doomed to a date with the crusher, the Futura lives on as the fuzzy-finished Batmobile and is still used for museum displays and shows across the United States.

1955 Mystere

Nineteen fifty-five was a big year for Ford show cars. The Mystere was one of the majority of nondriveable models to feature "stretch" ideas such as a rear engine compartment that could hold either a conventional or a turbine powerplant. This design, belonging primarily to designer Bill Boyer, was first shown to journalists by Design Vice President George Walker on October 5, 1955, in the Rotunda styling room. "It explores an entirely new, open feeling in styling," said Walker, "with complete integration of interior

and exterior styling." What it really did was give the public a look into the future of key styling cues that would be incorporated into the 1957 sedans, coupes and Thunderbirds. It actually wasn't shown to the public until 1956 for fear of giving away too much of what was to come in '57.

Driver and passengers entered the Mystere by raising the front half of the glass bubble canopy (hinged at the cowl) and opening

the swing-out doors. The back of the canopy was fixed. With the hot, clear-glass bubble, air conditioning was a must. The ignition featured a combination lock. The interior was equipped with a radio, and television for the rear seat passengers. The steering wheel could be positioned for either the right- or left-front seat positions. It was also one of the first vehicles to have dual headlamps, introduced across the

1955 Futura (Photo: Henry Ford Museum and Ford Motor Company)

1958 La Galaxie (Photo: Ford Motor Company)

board in all 1958 models. It shared a 52-inch height with the new Thunderbird. The wheelbase was 121 inches and the overall length stretched 220 inches.

1958 La Galaxie

Styling for 1958 cars in general was heavy-looking and the La Galaxie show car from Ford was no exception.

It was developed with window glass flush with the body panels and the most noted "design feature" of La Galaxie was a system that would keep the vehicle a safe distance from an object in front of it at speed on the highway. If the driver let La Galaxie get too close, the brakes would automatically apply and stop short of the object ahead.

This was, of course, only in the designer's mind, not a working part of the vehicle.

1958 E-196X

Another 1958 styling exercise was the E-196X, which would have been a vision of Edsel-like designs to come if the ill-fated vehicle had lasted beyond 1960. It sported a horse-collar grille nose as did almost all of the sketches of other possible versions of this model. Shown on opening page of this chapter is design chief George Walker (right) posing for a public relations photo to promote Ford's future vehicles.

▶

This right-hand drive Fairlane was somewhat unusual as high-line export models were not common. (Photo: Ford Motor Company)

KA 9363

FORD

Ford International in the Fifties

The 1956 Meteor was basically the '56 Ford but with Canadian trim to differentiate it from other cars. Only sold in Canada, the Meteor was the parallel to the Ford in the United States. Canada also sold the Monarch, comparable to the Mercury series.

Henry Ford's success with mass production of affordable vehicles depended on developing mass markets for them.

The major countries of Europe, South America and Asia were becoming lucrative markets for autos and trucks, but shipping them from the States was an expensive proposition.

Ford Motor Company had been exporting vehicles from the United States shortly after it began producing them, but it was clear that sending kits, known as KDs or knock downs, was necessary to allow export sales to countries that required local assembly to create employment. In some of the largest countries, Ford built manufacturing complexes, such as Brazil, where Model Ts were built.

This was the beginning of what would make Ford Motor Company one of the biggest powerhouses in the automotive industry for the next 100 years.

This also provided a stabilizing factor that kept the company running on an even keel. When profits were down on one continent, they were usually up somewhere else.

Brazil and Argentina

Ford Brazil started assembling vehicles in 1919 with a starting capital of $25,000. Opening operations in a rented warehouse in São Paulo, the ground floor was set up to assemble Model T cars from a boxed kit shipped in from the Ford Highland Park plant in Detroit. In 1925, the operation delivered almost 25,000 units from the São Paulo plant site and gained more interest from the Ford headquarters management.

Brazil later produced the Model A and then the V-8 Model B series from knocked-down kits. Brazil imported the Model Y and Anglia from England and the Ford Eifel from Germany during this period. The São Paulo plant was viewed by headquarters as quite industrious, building an average of 18,000 vehicles annually and even making their own wood parts for station wagons and trucks.

The post-war sedans were also assembled at São Paulo, but on

April 17, 1953, Ford opened a new plant at Ipiranga about an hour from the old site. While the São Paulo plant continued to produce the new Ford models for a hungry Brazilian market, on August 26, 1957, the company rolled the first Ford truck off the Ipiranga line, an F-600 model. The Ipiranga plant assembled 5,973 vehicles in its first year including the first Brazilian F-100 pickups. The trucks had 40 percent local content to meet government requirements.

The styling on the trucks followed a pattern Ford continues to this day. The Brazil operations always produced truck models that were a generation behind U.S. vehicles, receiving stamping and tooling handed down from the United States as North America began producing something new. The 1957 F-600 and F-100 Brazilian trucks were the same as the 1953 U.S. body styles. By 1959, Ford Brazil was building the equivalent of the North American '56 F-series trucks.

In 1959, Ford Brazil staged a cross-country trip from São Paulo to Vila Bela, considered by many to be impassable by vehicles. The purpose of the trip was to show the durability of F-600 trucks and also to gain the government's support in building a much-needed highway in Brazil to connect outer regions to the primary coastal cities. After twelve days of mud and 3,230 kilometers across Brazil's toughest terrain, the adventurers in their F-600s drove into Vila Bela, located in the midwestern part of Brazil just below the Amazon River.

The Pacheco Plant just north of Buenos Aires, Argentina, also was a progressive company, assembling and selling vehicles since 1925 for Argentines and customers in other South American countries. Argentina also built Ford sedans and, like Brazil, started building trucks in 1957. They came packaged for assembly from Detroit as knocked-down (KD) kits. Ford Argentina was turning in ample profits and at one point provided almost half of all the vehicles on the roads of that country.

Ford needed to tighten the grip on its facilities in Europe and determine what countries might show possibilities for future production. Spain, which demanded that all automobiles be completely manufactured, not just assembled there, was considered impractical. Over in Italy, Fiat had all the government-given advantages, leaving other manufacturers out in the cold. Other smaller countries—such as Finland, Sweden, Denmark and Belgium—all assembled parts shipped to them from Britain and sold cars through Ford sales offices within their countries.

Ford's major world manufacturing centers were located in Windsor, Canada; Dagenham, England; Poissy, France; Cologne, Germany; and the home site of Dearborn, Michigan. None of these sites coordinated their business actions with one another, so even though Ford owned businesses globally, each acted as a local business. Ford decided to form the International Division and named

Howard as vice president, with the assignment of centralizing foreign operations to coordinate their processes and bring the businesses closer together.

The Windsor, Canada, and Dagenham, England, operations were clearly the well-run Ford businesses outside of the United States. Much work needed to be done in France and Germany. Germany built a new manufacturing plant to launch the Taunus sedan, which proved popular beyond expectations. This helped put Cologne back on the map, bring in profits and start investing in its future. By the late 1950s, Ford of Germany began out-selling Ford of Britain.

In France, a bright young Dearborn executive, F. C. Reith, sold the Ford operation to Simca and then formed a Ford France sales operation to take the Simca-made, Ford-badged vehicles and sell them throughout France. Ford took about 15 percent of Simca's stock in trade for its operations, got rid of the headaches and still had Fords to sell.

Europe

After World War II, Henry Ford II took an ever-increasing interest in selling more cars in Europe. With much of Europe's auto industry recovering from the ravages of war, new cars were scarce. Customers on the continent and in Britain were eager to buy cars, and although none of Europe's countries would be buying in the volumes the United States was experiencing, the extra business could represent a substantial base for additional profits for Ford Motor Company.

In 1948, Henry and one of his executives specializing in international business, Graeme Howard, went to Europe to assess the situation and see what shape their facilities were in.

In 1957 Ford started advertising more of a global image. The company wanted the world to know that it built and sold Fords in many parts of the world. The 1958 advertising campaign furthered that effort by driving two sedans around the world, photographing them in well-known places along the way.

The right-hand drive '55 Ford models in New Zealand were imported from either Australia where they were assembled from kits, or directly from Canada.

Although the trim would be unfamiliar, an American could certainly feel at home with the continental kit.

Meteor side trim was substantially different, forming room for a three-tone paint job.

Canada

Canadian Fords in the 1950s were engineered and designed by Dearborn although they also sold variations of the U.S. models with unique styling. Canada sold regular U.S.-specification Fords and Mercurys but also the Monarch, which was a Mercury with Canadian trim, and the Meteor, which was a Ford with Canadian trim. The company made more than $17 million in 1949. Profits were apparently not where Henry thought they should be, so the entire operation was moved from Windsor to Toronto, starting production on May 11, 1953. A small-scale version of

Ford trucks teamed up to make a historic 12-day trip across Brazil in 1959 to prove the toughness of the vehicles and to bring national attention to the need of connecting major cities with good transportation routes. (Photo: Ford Motor Company)

1. New Thames Trader, by Ford of Britain   2. New Mercury M-600, by Ford of Canada (and U.S. export)   3. New Ford Ranchero, _and_ 4. Ford Styleside Pickup, by Ford of U.S. and Canada   5. New G-700, by Ford of Germany

Only new Ford-Built Trucks give you so much that's really new!

Thames Trader makes news— new, modern range of trucks! Choice of proven 4-cylinder or newly designed 6-cylinder petrol or diesel engines. Improved operating efficiency—greater payloads!

Mercury M-600 makes news— a rugged 2-tonner with boldly modern appearance . . . new, stronger frames, Heavy Duty V-8's, giant 19,500 lb. GVW.

The Ranchero makes news—more than a car, more than a truck. Has fine car lines, handles over 1000 lbs. payload.

Ford F-100 Styleside Pickup makes news with the biggest pickup bodies ever built—up to 70 cu. ft., 5,000 lb. GVW.

G-700 makes news with new automatic four-wheel drive for positive acceleration, improved climbing ability.

New 1957 Ford-built trucks feature the most sweeping changes in truck history. They not only _look_ like the world's most modern trucks— _they are!_ Changes in design make them more economical than ever to run and to maintain.

Wherever you live . . . you get more for your money in any Ford-built product

Ford-built products include cars, trucks, tractors, industrial engines, genuine replacement parts: Meteor • Monarch / Popular • Anglia • Prefect • Consul • Zephyr • Zodiac • Thames • Fordson Major Tractor / Taunus • FK Truck / Continental Mark II • Lincoln • Mercury • Ford • Thunderbird • Ford Tractor and Implements

In this international truck ad, Ford was making an effort at showing the world its "global-ness." This ad pictures a Thames Trader from England, a Mercury M-600 from Canada, F-100 and Ranchero from Canada and the U.S., and the G-700 commercial truck from Ford in Germany.

Other than right-hand drive, New Zealand-bound cars were basically the same as the U.S. models. This '57 station wagon was the Country Sedan version with a dealer add-on exterior sun visor.

Dearborn's headquarters building was built. The manufacturing facilities to produce cars and trucks for Canada also built vehicles shipped in knocked-down kit form to Australia and New Zealand. At that point, Windsor became an engine-manufacturing facility for assembly plants throughout North America.

Australia and New Zealand

In 1949, Australia was receiving vehicles from both England and the United States. England was

This unique 1955 model was an Australian "UTE," or utility vehicle. These car-based pickups have been popular down-under since the 1940s.

shipping in the Pilot, a V-8 Sedan mostly assembled in England. There were often some partially knocked-down Pilots sent to dealers for assembly in Australia. New Zealand imported both Australian- and Canadian-made vehicles. Prior to 1949, the Fords coming in from the United States were the pre-war design, with transverse springs and flathead V-8 engines. Chevy and Chrysler were already selling models with independent front suspensions and overhead-valve six-cylinder engines.

When the new 1949 Ford sedans began making their way into Australia, everyone was excited until they realized that these vehicles simply were not built for harsh Australian roads. City drivers had no problems with the new independent front suspension, but a driver from the Outback would carry extra shock absorbers and replace them on the road every 300 kilometers as the rubber bushings wore out! By 1954, Australia was assembling the British Prefect, but in 1955 they started production of the Mainline and Customline series from the United States with Dearborn's new overhead-valve V-8 engine.

Most of the cars Ford built in Australia were the base models, sold both there and in New Zealand.

This 1957 dash was from a stripped model with only a radio option.

In the Mercury section of the 1953 Canadian Auto Show, the scale model of the Muroc concept car was prominently displayed. (Photo: David Warman Collection)

Mercury trucks were sold only in Canada and all came with V-8 engines—no 6-cylinders.

The dash of the '58 Australian Ford was similar to the American models, and the radio had a different layout. The shifter was on the left side of the steering column or it would have hit the door.

In New Zealand Ford for 1959 matched the U.S. models, only with the usual right-hand-drive setup.

Henry Ford II made his first visit to Brazil in 1959 to see the recently opened Ipiranga Assembly Plant where the Brazilian Ford trucks were first produced in October 1957. The body style for Brazil's 1957 F-Series was the same as the North American 1953 models.

The 1963 model Thunderbird was the last in this three-year series. Thunderbird continued to grow in size with each new design release and '64 would be no exception. (Photo: Ford Motor Company)

This also was the first Ford sold in Australia with automatic transmission. Although doing well, selling 42,968 vehicles in 1955, Ford was still far behind Holden's (General Motors') 50 percent share of the market.

That same year, Ford Australia received funding to start building the Broadmeadows Assembly facilities outside of Melbourne to produce the Zephyr. The Mainline and Customline models of the mid-1950s were all right-hand drive, many completely assembled when they arrived and some with assembly to be done in Australia.

Ford managed, since the beginning almost, to sell cars globally. The Model T made the Ford name famous around the world. Ford cars in the 1950s were stylish and rolling out the doors in North America by the millions.

Most of the other operations simply imported cars to dealers or received KD kits for local assembly. However it was done, in most corners of the world, the Ford name was well known and Ford cars and trucks were a part of the culture.

FORD

Ford Prepares for a New Decade

Probably the biggest news and success for Ford in the '60s was Mustang. The first model was released to the public on April 17, 1964, and designated a 1964 1/2 model. More than 121,000 Mustangs were sold in the five-month run before the September introduction of the 1965 models. (Photo: Ford Motor Company)

The 1950s started off in an uncertain manner, but with the leadership of Henry Ford II and Ernie Breech, Ford was soon climbing up the manufacturing ladder. Although there were years when the market was not as healthy, the decade was good to Ford and with the help of key management there were excellent profits and millions of cars and trucks. They overtook Chevrolet in 1957 but slipped back to second place again in 1958, a tough sales year for everyone.

As Robert McNamara, Henry Ford II and Ernie Breech looked to 1960, they were facing the challenge of delivering all new body styles for the sedans, convertibles and wagons and the long-awaited small car, the Falcon. The Fords of the fifties were industry leaders with style and innovative engineering firsts. Their post-war body design was six months ahead of Chevy and the Ford overhead valve V-8 was running in new Fords a year before its chief competitor introduced one. After coming close to extinction in the mid-forties, Ford was now brimming with talented management and exciting new products.

With money in the bank and more over-the-top products on the horizon, the company took a big step into the sixties.

Ford would be building large and small cars in multiple model lines, ranging from the Falcon, Fairlanes and Galaxie 500s to the Mustang that created a totally new segment for the automotive industry.

Lee Iacocca would move up from his regional sales office to head one of the world's largest car divisions during a period of "Total Performance" in sales and motorsports.

Auto racing legends such as Fireball Roberts and Fred Lorenzen would join Ford and the Holman-Moody team to leave a permanent mark on NASCAR.

When he couldn't buy Ferrari, Henry the Deuce would commit a great amount of Ford money to the development of a Ford sports car to win both LeMans and the World

Manufacturers' Championship.

The sixties would see Whiz Kids, now matured to senior management, bring Ford Motor Company into the new decade— a special era consisting of an up-and-down economy, great motor racing and the Vietnam war, protesters and flower children.

There would also be some serious sales competition coming from Asia in the form of small, well-built Toyotas and Datsuns that would forever change the way American companies built and sold their products.

The new decade would be a time of competition like Detroit had never seen and also a time of growth in learning about new processes in manufacturing, building for quality and running a more efficient business.

Fords of the sixties would be an exciting decade—one of fast cars, great design and tough competition.

Lee Iacocca (right) and vice president of engineering Stu Frey pose beside two key elements of Ford's success in the sixties—the 1960 Falcon and the 1964 ½ Mustang. (Photo: Ford Motor Company)

The 1967 Fairlane GT-A, equipped with automatic transmission and a 390 cubic inch engine, was competition for Pontiac's GTO and Oldsmobile's 442 factory hot rods. (Photo: Ford Motor Company)

Thunderbird design for 1961 was a complete break from the past "square birds," keeping it well separated from any other Ford line. With a $4170 base price, the new model sold only 62,000 units, much less than the previous year's model. (Photo: Ford Motor Company)

The all-new styling of the 1960 Starliner carried the only 2-door hardtop in the Ford lineup. More than 68,000 of this model were sold at a base price of $2723. (Photo: Ford Motor Company)

By 1963 Ford was making many advances in both design and quality. The new Fastback roofline for the '63 model Galaxie was introduced shortly after the first of the year partially for styling purposes but also to support a sleeker NASCAR entry. This is the model that swept the top three spots at the Daytona 500 that year with Tiny Lund winning. (Photo: Ford Motor Company)

Note: *Page numbers in bold indicate photograph or illustration.*